FASHION IS OUR BUSINESS

FASHION IS OUR BUSINESS

BY

BERYL (WILLIAMS) EPSTEIN

° CLARE POTTER ° EMILY WILKENS °
° HATTIE CARNEGIE ° CLAIRE McCARDELL °
° NORMAN NORELL ° JO COPELAND °
° PHILIP MANGONE ° EDITH HEAD °
° LOUELLA BALLERINO ° MARISKA KARASZ °
° MABS ° VORIS °

Essay Index Reprint Series

BOOKS FOR LIBRARIES PRESS
FREEPORT, NEW YORK

INTERNATIONAL STANDARD BOOK NUMBER:

0-8369-1920-3

LIBRARY OF CONGRESS CATALOG CARD NUMBER:

72-117787

PRINTED IN THE UNITED STATES OF AMERICA

CONTENTS

Contents

FASHION IS OUR BUSINESS

ONE

—————YOU ARE INTERESTED————— IN CLOTHES

Let's take for granted right from the start that you and I both think clothes are pretty exciting. You wouldn't be reading this book if you didn't, and I wouldn't have written it.

Let's even assume that you think they're exciting in a serious way—that your interest in clothes is deeper than a magpie-ish desire to own a lot of them, and a tendency to regard a dress simply and solely as something to make you prettier. (Not that every one of your dresses shouldn't do that for you; it should. But I hope you don't own a frock, no matter how becoming it is, which won't wear reasonably well, and which doesn't fit into the program of your needs and the rest of your wardrobe.)

If you have a real sense of clothes you ask yourself *why* a specific dress is becoming or isn't, and why you feel somehow right in it, or completely wrong. If you're farther along than that—if you've trained yourself at all—perhaps you even know the answers to those questions.

You know, for example, that a dress is not automatically becoming to you because it's what "they're wearing." There are girls who should never be seen outside their own rooms in a pleated skirt. If you've got the sort of hips that pleated skirts mold into a minor catastrophe, and you persist in wearing pleated skirts anyway—well, then, your interest in clothes isn't what you'd call very well developed.

Or if a round neckline does bad things for your face, and you go right out and buy a dress with a round neckline because your best friend is wearing one—*that's* not being serious about clothes either.

But you're not that kind. You've already made a fair start at analyzing yourself—not a very easy job if you're still growing or otherwise changing shape almost daily. When you buy or make a new dress you put your whole mind on it, and the results are apparent. And—this is also important—you're interested in what your friends wear, too, and in all the clothes that you see around you on the street and at school. In other words, you *react* to clothes, whether they're yours or someone else's.

If I've described you correctly so far, I'll probably be safe in saying one more thing about you: you rather think, although of course you may not be at all sure yet, that the career you choose for yourself will have something to do with clothes.

It has occurred to you that you might like to be a designer.

If that thought has occurred to you more than once, you are the sort of girl I had in mind when I decided to write this book.

You are Interested in Clothes

Now of course you've probably read several books on the subject of fashion and fashion design, or you intend to. And goodness knows there are numerous books to read. There are books on the history of dress through the ages; there are books on textiles and fabrics; there are books on sewing and draping and fitting; there are books that will teach you how to put your fashion ideas on paper. There are also books that are intended to advise you on the subjects you might most wisely study, together with suggestions about the best schools specializing in the teaching of design. The catalogues of those schools make good reading in themselves, if your enthusiasm is really pretty far developed.

You may reasonably ask, then, why—if there are already in existence such volumes as I've referred to—why *this* book is being written.

It's because I think you may be wondering, not only about fashion, but about fashion designers themselves.

Once, of course, such artists were virtually the personal servants of queens and royal ladies, catering to their whims alone, and only incidentally—because of the widespread influence of their mistresses—guiding the fashions of the world. Then they became more independent and, in the early days of this century, they were themselves the czar-like rulers of what fashionable women wore. They handed down their dictates with little regard for what their clients might actually like or be comfortable in; and the relatively few women who could afford their clothes accepted slavishly what they were sold.

Nowadays the status of designers has changed again, because their customers have changed. Those customers have learned to think for themselves about clothes, and have come to the conclusion that things should be wearable as well as a badge of one's ability to "keep in style." And those customers now include, not just the noble-blooded or the very wealthy, but—because of the development of the wholesale ready-to-wear industry—all women, everywhere.

So American designers today, although they are vital, imaginative personalities in themselves, are more than that. As a professional group they are the sensitive, intelligent reflectors of what American women want them to be, creating what American women want to wear.

You can, naturally, learn a good deal about them through their work, either by reading about it in fashion magazines or newspaper columns, or by seeing it with your own eyes; for after all, their work is a form of self-expression, as all art is. But there is a lot that their work can't tell you. It seldom suggests, for example, whether they went to designing schools or were taught their business in some other way . . . or what they were like when they were your age, and how old they were when they first became as interested in clothes as you are today . . . and what happened to them after they finished school—whether they got wonderful jobs the very next day and saw their creations featured in *Vogue* a few months later, or whether it was a long and difficult climb.

This book will, I hope, satisfy your curiosity on such things, at least in regard to the representative group of twelve designers discussed in its pages. It will, in other words, introduce them to you, informally, as I met them myself.

You'll probably like them. You'll certainly feel that they have a great deal in common with you. After all, they like clothes too. And the generous cooperation they gave in the preparation of this book is an indication of their good will toward all of you who share their principal interest.

You'll find that their backgrounds vary widely. They were, as a matter of fact, selected from among the country's outstanding designers largely because they traveled such markedly different paths toward a similar goal. (And this is as good a place as any to confess that I wish there were room in the book for dozens more—not only from New York and California, but from such other cities as St. Louis and Boston, which are rapidly taking their place as important centers of the country's clothing industry.) Some of them had formal education in designing, and some of them learned by a sort of apprentice method. Some of them were supported by their families while they studied, and some began to support themselves when they were scarcely more than children. Some of them intended right from the start to be designers, and others aimed at quite different careers and are rather surprised to find themselves where they are. Some of them had a lot of good luck on the way, and some of them had very little.

As a matter of fact, there is only one statement that can truthfully be made about all of them: they all worked extremely hard, and with tremendous concentration; and although they are all successful, none of them had success handed over on a platter. You may even feel, after you've met them in these chapters, that you don't want to be a designer after all, if it's as difficult as it appears. It is. Almost every one of these designers will assure you of that.

But read about them now for yourselves. It is their hope and mine that this book will help you to make up your mind about your own career; that it may offer you at least a hint of what your life may be like if you do become a successful designer, and more than a hint of what you may expect to experience along the road.

TWO

CLARE POTTER

The lobby at 550 Seventh Avenue, in New York City, is always crowded. And although the people hurrying through it might be any assortment of city dwellers, for they are male and female, young and not-so-young, prosperous looking and otherwise, they have one thing in common. They are all a part of that great network called the women's apparel industry.

Within the surrounding few blocks are dozens of other buildings, devoted, like 550 Seventh Avenue, to the manufacturing and selling of coats and suits and dresses. But 550 is perhaps the most representative and the most exciting of all. The big directory on the wall reads like a list of advertisers in *Vogue*.

So, on my first visit there, I was tempted to begin at the beginning and explore. But I had an appointment to keep, and consequently I squeezed firmly into one of the several elevators, and squeezed out again a few seconds later at the sixteenth floor and Charles W. Nudelman, Inc.

The reception room I found myself in was plain and businesslike. Behind a glass partition two girls and a man checked order slips as prosaically as if they dealt in nuts and bolts rather than in some of the most glamorous clothes in the world. One of them took my name and told me to wait.

And then a friendly voice said, "Hello," and Clare Potter was standing in the doorway at the end of the hall. "Come on in," she said.

Perhaps the first of the American designers to become generally known to the public, Clare Potter wears her recognition as easily and casually as she wore the bow-tied blue blouse and navy skirt she had on. A fat red heart-shaped pincushion dangling handily from her waist was simultaneous evidence of hard work and good humor. She was slender, with nice slender, capable-looking hands. And her dark hair lay smoothly on either side of a face that managed to appear serene and amused, at one and the same time.

The moment I had followed her through a heavy wood door, Charles W. Nudelman, Inc. ceased to resemble an ordinary business office. Now I was in a brief passageway where pale walls made an effective background for vivid color photographs of Clare Potter designs that had been featured in the glossy fashion magazines. A moment later, in Mrs. Potter's office, there were the same pale walls and more of those beautiful pictures.

The designer sat down at an immaculate pale wood desk, and asked immediately what sort of a book I was writing, and why. While I told her about it she sounded interested—*really* interested, as I discovered later she sounded about most things.

CLARE POTTER

THE CLEAR, SINGING TONES OF
AN APPARENTLY LIMITLESS PALETTE DISTINGUISH CLARE
POTTER'S FLOWING, ALMOST CLASSICALLY SIMPLE CLOTHES.
SHE INSISTS SHE DOESN'T INVENT COLORS—THAT SHE
MERELY "SEES" THEM.

KAY BELL

NO BLACK=AND=WHITE PICTURE
CAN DO JUSTICE TO A CLARE POTTER DRESS, BUT IT CAN
ILLUSTRATE THE SIMPLICITY OF LINE AND CUT WITH WHICH
SHE MANIPULATES HER EXQUISITELY DYED FABRICS.

And when I had finished she said, "But then you don't just want to sit around here and talk, do you? Wouldn't you rather go inside to the workroom?"

Of course I would, and I knew that you too would want to know what a designer's workroom looks like. So I followed her through the big showroom, where buyers from stores and specialty shops all over the country gather two or three times a year to see the season's "collection." Here again the colors were subdued. Chairs of pale wood upholstered in oatmeal-colored cloth stood around the edge of a huge expanse of pale carpet. At one side was a small platform, with stage entrances for the parading models. The whole room had clearly been designed as an elegantly unobtrusive frame for the clothes which were displayed there.

And then we went through another heavy door, and suddenly we were really behind the scenes. No longer was the atmosphere quiet and subdued. It was noisy with the sound of whirring machines, and bright with heaps of material and half-finished garments hanging everywhere.

I opened my mouth to say, "Why, this looks just like a factory!" But I stopped myself in time.

Of course it did. And I realized I shouldn't have been surprised. It *was* a factory.

And for the first time all the information I had heard and read about American designers became real to me. They are, with very few exceptions, parts—though very important parts, of course—of manufacturing plants that turn out goods in wholesale quantities. They aren't temperamental creatures, dreaming in an ivory tower over a drawing board or a length of material. They don't make *a dress*. They, together with the production lines of which they are units, make thousands of dresses.

I was to become increasingly aware of that as my acquaintance with designers grew, but at the moment I had no time for more than a startled realization of the factory itself. We were hurrying through the corner of a big room, through another smaller room—full of more machines and more people—and then we turned into the smallest room of all.

"Find a place to sit down," Mrs. Potter said. "Here. Use my desk." She scooped a couple of books and a bolt of cloth from the plain wooden chair behind it. "And I'll just go on with what I was doing."

This was really her desk. Small and scarred and heaped with a variety of articles, it was about as unlike that beautiful piece of furniture in her outer office as it could possibly be. And now I knew why that other one had appeared so neat and uncluttered. I suspected that it was never used at all, except on rare occasions when Mrs. Potter sat down before it and then, a moment later—as she had done with me—got up again to depart for her workroom.

When I was settled, had found a place for my purse on the already crowded sill of the single window, and tucked my feet on the chair rung to get them out of the way, I looked around.

The room was perhaps ten feet wide and half again as long, so that even the small desk and chair took up a good portion of it. Over my head, on the wall, was a shelf of books —books on costume design and art, mostly.

The other half of the room consisted chiefly of a small raised platform, surrounded on three sides by mirrors. A girl stood on the platform when we came in, wearing a half-finished dress, and Mrs. Potter went to her and sat down on the edge of the platform to study the dress, first looking up at it, then looking at it in the mirror.

"Let's see. Turn around, will you?" she murmured.

There was a great sheaf of clothes hanging beside the doorway. I couldn't see their details, because they had been placed too close together, but the colors of them made a vivid splash of light. There was color all over the room. I had seen the clothes first, because they were closest to where I sat. But now, everywhere I looked, color was what I saw. Bolts of glowing yellow and frosted green leaned drunkenly in a corner, bolts of clear blue and soft rose stood on a shelf, little swatches of various hues scattered the desk in front of me.

Even if I had never seen a dress that Clare Potter designed, I could have guessed from the sight of this room, why fashion and advertising writers spoke, as they so often did, of "Clare

FASHION IS OUR BUSINESS

Potter, colorist . . ." "Clare Potter, whose genius with color . . ."

"No. I don't like that at all."

Mrs. Potter had risen quickly to her feet, and was bending down to remove with quick, deft fingers a broad band of green that had been pinned to the hem of the half-completed evening dress the blonde model wore.

"It wasn't right, was it?"

She looked up at the girl in the dress, and then over at another model who had perched to rest on the window sill.

"Not quite, somehow," the second one agreed.

"It seemed like a fine idea when I thought of it," the designer explained to the room at large, "but you can't tell about things until you actually try them. There." The green band was off. "At least it looks less like a lampshade now. I'll have to get rid of the green at the waist, too. Now let me see."

She stood back to study the dress again. It was of soft white jersey, patterned in a sort of Victorian wallpaper design of splashy pink roses and green leaves. The waist was simple, almost severe, with reveres folded back at the neck. The skirt, shirred into a band, fell in soft folds.

"Green would be fine—if it were the right green," Mrs. Potter murmured. She pushed away a handful of papers that hid the telephone, and called the stockroom. Did the stockroom have a grosgrain material in a soft dark moss green? she inquired. No, the stockroom didn't. Then what about—?

She eyed the dress once more, through narrowed lids. Wine? Yes, wine might be just the thing. The petals of the roses in the print deepened to wine at their base. "Send it up, will you, please?"

While she was waiting for it, she had time to tell me about her own particular method of designing. She doesn't sketch first, as many do. She works her ideas out directly on the figure, cutting and draping, pinning and basting, in the material in which the actual dress is to be made.

"That's because I depend so much upon texture, and the way a material hangs," she said. "Some designers make a muslin model first, of course, but muslin is stiff and it doesn't give the same impression as a softer fabric—especially when the model wearing the dress is walking or moving. And after all, you want to know how a dress is going to look when the woman wearing it is in motion. People don't just stand still. Of course it's an extravagant way to work, but—" she smiled and looked so young that her next words were surprising—"but I've been in this business nearly fifteen years, and I've learned not to be too wasteful."

Asked if she had made up her mind when she was a child that she was going to be a designer, she smiled again.

"It never occurred to me. I intended to be an artist. I just took that for granted."

She talked about her childhood then, and it sounded ordinary and healthy and pleasant. Her family lived in Jersey City, New Jersey, right across the Hudson River from New

FASHION IS OUR BUSINESS

York. Clare—she was Clare Meyer then—had one sister, enough older than she so that they didn't play much together, but Clare didn't miss companionship. She liked, even at an early age, to do things on her own. When she was small they were likely to be rather tomboyish things, and later on, by the time she was in high school, they frequently assumed the form of money-making endeavors.

"I was always taking jobs," she says. "I didn't have to—that is, we didn't need the money, and it wasn't my family's idea. I just liked to. One vacation I worked at a telephone exchange, and another time I did clerical work. I had jobs in department stores too, and I learned a lot that way that has been helpful to me since. And all the jobs, of course, taught me to discipline myself. That's something that most youngsters don't learn in school, and they have to learn it somewhere."

Her high school art teacher took an interest in her, and by the time she was fifteen Clare was attending classes at the Art Students' League, hurrying in to New York for them after school. And when she finished high school, she attended Pratt Institute in Brooklyn.

She still had every intention of becoming an artist. But one day the director of the Institute called her aside and asked her if she had ever thought about studying costume design. She knew Clare made her own clothes, and she thought they indicated a distinctive feeling for color and line—far more so, she suggested tactfully, than Clare's portraits and landscapes did.

"Really, my pictures were very bad," Clare says now, reminiscently. "I didn't think so then, of course, but the director was so wonderful—arranging for me to go directly into a designing course, without taking the usual year of sewing first—that I agreed to her plan. I took some special outside work at a draping school, in order to catch up, and began to study designing.

"Maybe it was because I wasn't much good and they wanted to get rid of me, or maybe it was because I was still trying to do things on my own and my ideas didn't always fit into the school's program—anyhow, for some reason Pratt found a job for me before I had finished the course. They sent me to work for Edward L. Mayer, who was a very important dress manufacturer."

It was in the period when the most fashionable materials were those elaborately embroidered in silk and tiny beads, and Clare's job was to create designs for the embroidery.

"It was so easy that I was simply amazed to be paid for it," she says. "I couldn't believe that just going to museums and looking at a lot of pictures, and then getting an idea and drawing it, was actually *work*. I began to suggest new ways to make up the dresses, too, and Mr. Mayer liked some of them. So pretty soon I found out I was designing clothes."

Of course it wasn't all easy. She remained at that house for three years, learning a great deal about the business of dress manufacturing as well as the pleasure of planning dresses. When she left she spent six months in Mexico, returned to New York and worked for a while in another wholesale house, and finally took the job she holds now, with Charles W. Nudelman.

The boy from the stockroom arrived and conversation was immediately suspended. He had brought the wine-colored grosgrain and another new bolt of cloth—a vivid yellow patterned with small black insects. He had liked it so well when it arrived that he had thought Mrs. Potter would want to see it right away.

She liked it too, very much. Everybody exclaimed over the yellow material for some time.

"You know, even the stockroom people here take a tremendous interest in what goes on," the designer confided when he had gone, apparently unaware that her own enthusiasm for colors was contagious and as likely an explanation for others' interest as the beauty of materials themselves. "I can always tell how they feel about things, even if they don't say a word. If they like something, they talk about it. And if they have to bring in something they don't like, they just drop it"—she illustrated with a disdainful gesture—"without a word."

The wine color was exactly right. Stockroom boy, models and designer had agreed about that. So Mrs. Potter began to cut and pin a waistband to cover up the last trace of that unsuccessful green.

"And of course the people out there," she went on, nodding over her shoulder toward the room beyond her own cubby hole, "make no attempt at all to keep their opinions to themselves. If they don't like something I do, they let me know about it in no uncertain terms."

The "people out there"—four men and two women—constituted the "sample" staff. It was their job to make up finished garments duplicating Clare's pinned and basted models. First they made a paper pattern, then they cut the dress itself from the pattern and made it up, leaving Clare's own original intact as a guide. Their job finished, the dress was studied again, any necessary changes agreed upon, and then—if it was considered satisfactory—it was added to the collection ready to be shown to customers. Additional patterns had to be made for a successful dress, of course, in all the various sizes; and, as orders came in, it could then be made up in quantity lots for shipment to stores in every corner of the country.

"Our factory is right on the premises. Come on—I'll show you," Mrs. Potter said suddenly. "You rest a while," she added to the model.

"They're all wonderful workmen," she said a moment later, as we walked up and down between the long rows of men and women at work at machines in the big room. There were piles of finished and unfinished work beside each one. Some people were sewing seams, others were binding them. Some were making buttonholes. They looked up to smile briefly at her, without ceasing their work, and she seemed to know all of them by name.

"You don't like doing that, do you, John?" she smiled at one man who was performing the tedious job of stitching around the circumference of fat appliquéd dots.

He grinned. "I don't mind. If I don't have to do it too long."

The supervisor of the workroom explained a little later that he saw to it that John and the others were never allowed to do any one thing "too long."

"We cut out, say, five hundred dresses at a time," he said, "but we don't make them all up at once. They'd get bored."

He and the workmen and Mrs. Potter talked together with an air of mutual respect, all of them aware that good, well-made clothes resulted only from a complete cooperation. It hadn't occurred to me before, but it did now, that a designer has to be able to understand not only the people she works *for*—her customers, the women who wear her clothes—but also the people she works *with*.

We looked in at the long racks of garments awaiting shipment, in an adjoining room, and then Mrs. Potter introduced me to the owner of the company.

"Mr. Nudelman has been in the business since 1901," she explained. "He was just a boy then, looking for a job. And while he was walking along the street one day, his hat blew off and the wind carried it through a shop door. There was a sign on the window saying, 'Boy Wanted.' So he followed his hat inside and asked for the job. It happened to be a clothing shop—and he's been in the business ever since."

Mr. Nudelman's round face beamed when he talked about American designers. "They haven't had enough opportunity yet," he said, "but when they're given the chance they can do wonderful things. Mrs. Potter has gone to Paris on pleasure trips, but she agrees with me that it's better not even to go inside the Paris dress houses to look at the collections there."

"That's right, I do." The designer nodded. "I don't like to see too many clothes, ever. It's so easy to be influenced, and to lose whatever individuality you possess. I get my ideas from all sorts of places, but I'm afraid that if I tried to get them from other people's dresses, I'd begin to design things that were only adaptations of what I'd seen. The Paris influence used to be too pervasive, I think—it affected everybody and they all turned out clothes that showed its mark. I don't think we should ever let that happen again."

"American designers know the sort of clothes American women want to wear," Mr. Nudelman pointed out, "and they can make them, too. Women used to think they had to go to Paris for their clothes, or buy copies of Paris models here, because it was the thing to do. But the war changed that. They discovered that they can be just as happy and just as well-dressed without depending on Paris at all. And, in my opinion, women began to be better-dressed than they had ever been before, when designers here *couldn't* go to Paris."

He talked for a while about the whole ready-to-wear dress industry, as he had seen it develop during the past twenty-five years. He pointed out that it had started as a business rather than as a large-scale reproduction of fine clothes, and that only recently were designers beginning to receive proper recognition in the field.

"And lots of them don't have it yet," he added. "Manufacturers are still influenced by the days when they did nothing but copy French models. They're afraid to give our own designers the credit they deserve—maybe," he grinned, "because they're afraid the designers will want more money if they get it. But if a designer is good, she—or he—deserves a fair share of the profits a manufacturer makes."

Mr. Nudelman practices what he preaches about the value of recognizing American designers. Clare Potter was one of the first young Americans to become well-known to the public by name, and Mr. Nudelman was pleased rather than annoyed when customers began to ask for Clare Potter frocks.

Back in her own workroom Mrs. Potter studied a pair of black lounging pajamas. Broad stripes down the front of the trousers were in shades of pale yellow and green, and the tucked-in blouse was simplicity itself. They were a striking representative of a type of clothes for which she is particularly famous. Before Mrs. Potter went to work on lounging pajamas, those garments were likely to be either blatantly comfortable, or fussily decorated. The air of sophistication she gave them was new, and vastly welcome to many women. She gives that same air of sophistication to simple sports clothes too.

"Yes," she nodded now decisively, "they're all right. I don't think they need another thing."

And as the model retired to the long-mirrored dressing room, planned for the girls' comfort as carefully as the make-up room of a theater, she smiled at her retreating back.

"She likes that outfit," she said. "She feels good in it. We keep our models here all the year around, and I make my clothes right on them. Each garment not only fits one particular girl, but is her *sort* of dress."

The models were of different types—tall and dark, honey blonde and pale blonde—and each of them wore clothes that were becoming to her, and would be becoming to other women of her coloring and characteristics.

By studying the girls carefully, by listening to the comments of her customers from all over the country, and by traveling a good deal herself, Mrs. Potter gets a very real feeling of the clothes that women need.

"A housewife in Texas isn't going to want the same clothes that a New York businesswoman buys," she points out, "and you have to get around and find out what it is each of them needs."

In general, she explained, she designs on the principle that

FASHION IS OUR BUSINESS

American women are active and busy and want day-time clothes that will stand up under any conditions; and that when they have time to relax, they want to be gay and pretty as well as comfortable. So she gives them that kind of clothes, all turned out in her unmistakable manner.

She likes easy-flowing lines, and no trimmings that are "stuck on" to detract from the almost classically simple designs of most of her clothes. In one collection the only noticeably "stuck on" trimming was a pair of vivid flowers at the waistline of an otherwise extremely plain, fitted tunic worn over silk trousers, for lounging and dinner at home. The charm of even her most expensive evening dresses relies on clarity of line and beauty of color, rather than upon an elaboration of cut or decoration. Necklines and sleeves are simple too, and often a soft tied drapery is a frock's only trimming.

But she lets herself go with colors. Working most frequently with plain, unpatterned materials, she combines two and sometimes three blending or contrasting shades with an ability that seems peculiarly her own. One store that carries her clothes said of her, characteristically, that "simplicity is her touchstone, color her magic." And indeed it seems to be true. Color is the thing that comes first to mind when her clothes are mentioned, just as color had been what first struck the eye in her workroom.

How does she achieve the apparently boundless variety of shades that distinguish her collections? Does she sit puddling about for hours on end with paints, mixing in a little of that and a little of this until she hits upon a new and striking shade?

"No," she laughed, "it's not so complicated. I just see something I like—and have it copied by a textile manufacturer. See? I cut a piece out of this, because I thought it was pretty and I might want to make use of it." And she pointed to the vivid blue mailing label pasted to a manila envelope lying on her cluttered desk. There was a neat rectangular hole in the label's center.

Once, she explained, she brought back several tins of paint from a Bermuda vacation; they were intended to be used to decorate a powder room, but she liked them so well—"You know the colors of the houses there," she smiled; "how soft and glowing they are"—that she had many of them made up into materials, and they started a vogue for Bermuda shades that swept the country. And once she found a vivid rose in the paper of a memo pad, and she used that too.

I asked if her visit to Mexico had influenced her a good deal.

"Of course." She nodded. "I was there for six months, and that's a long time out of anybody's life; it couldn't help but leave some impression on me. But as to the colors—well, the colors I saw there weren't the same colors most people see, I guess. People are always telling me that the colors in Mexico are so vivid and crude. The ones I noticed seemed to me very sophisticated and subtle. Everybody has pretty much the same eyes, I suppose; but they see different things with them."

And that seems to be her secret—if you can call it a secret. She just *sees* colors, and adopts them.

"And now let's see how *you* look." She turned to another model wearing a slack suit of softest chocolate brown, with a pale blue waist band and a pink brassière top showing at the opening of the brief bolero. "Mmm. All right. And you'll wear brown shoes with it, and a blue band in your hair. There shouldn't be any other pink but that one spot. Go show it to the boys. See how they like it."

The model wandered out, smiling, to the pattern room, and Mrs. Potter smiled too.

"You know, we don't have any salesmen here," she said. "When we have our showings for buyers, Mr. Nudelman and I talk to the customers for the first few days, and then the girls take over. They know the clothes and they like them. The clothes are *theirs*. And they can talk about them better than anybody else could."

And then suddenly everybody became aware that it was five o'clock. The models hurried off, the machines stopped in the pattern room and in the big room beyond, and the designer herself prepared to leave for her farm in West Nyack, N. Y., across the river from Manhattan. There, she explained, as she took off her dangling pincushion and powdered her nose, there she and her husband raise Dalmatian dogs and ride their own horses. And she added parenthetically that she had had a successful print made after a Dalmatian's spottings, and that she had just recently suggested to a textile designer that it might be a good idea to print tiny black horses on a soft grey jersey. They garden in West Nyack, too, although she didn't recall having transferred any of her vegetables to a length of fabric.

On the whole, she pointed out, she still likes the out-of-doors activities she liked as a child, and she still likes to do things for herself. Probably that latter admission explains why her designs are so distinctive, and why she avoids any influences that would make them less so. And perhaps it is for that same reason that, although she does not wear all her own models herself, she is the sort of woman to whom, according to one fashion writer, Clare Potter clothes are most becoming—"the assured, aware woman."

She is both of those things—assured in her talent; and aware not only of the world about her, as all creative people must be, but of her own place in the industry of which she is an independent but cooperating part.

In 1937 Clare Potter received the Lord & Taylor award for distinguished designing in the field of sports for women, and two years later she received the award given by the big Dallas, Texas, store, Nieman-Marcus, for distinguished service in the field of fashion. Such awards are gratifying, of course, but it is her work itself that she obviously enjoys more than any honors it brings her. And her pleasure in what she does is evident in each of her designs, flowing with movement and singing with color.

In the opinion of a great many people—including thousands of women who happily wear her clothes—Clare Potter, in spite of her own denial, has amply fulfilled her childhood ambition to be an artist.

THREE

━━━━━EMILY WILKENS━━━━━

Thousands of teen-age girls who feel well-dressed and attractive today in Emily Wilkens' clothes, used to be pretty unhappy about the things they had to choose from in their local stores. They were limited—and unfairly, they thought—to either the dresses in the children's departments, which their mothers usually wanted them to wear but which they themselves thought were too babyish; or to the junior-miss models, which offered them the styles they wanted—although they seldom fit—but which their mothers thought were too grown-up. And then Emily Wilkens came along. She could still remember back to the days, not so long before, when she was a teen-ager herself and not very happy; and she decided to do something about what she felt were the very special clothes problems of that age. Her success is a matter of record—and a matter for gratification to her young customers everywhere.

Emily was born in Hartford, Connecticut, in 1918, and she began to worry about clothes very shortly afterward. Her father was a well-to-do real estate man, so her worries weren't financial. And Emily was the oldest in a family of four, so it wasn't a case of hand-me-downs either. But she was small for her age, and had to wear a size six dress when she was eight; and as early as that she found it infuriating to look so much younger than she felt, and so—so *bunchy*, besides. To make matters worse, she had a friend who was remarkably pretty, and who always seemed to look wonderful no matter what she put on. Emily thought it wasn't fair. She thought her clothes ought somehow help her to look that way too, instead of just making her look worse.

Mrs. Wilkens' hands were quick and clever, and she made her daughter beautiful little knitted coats and suits; but you can't wear knitted clothes all the time, and Emily had plenty of opportunities to suffer in ready-mades that she didn't like.

The trunkful of dresses that an affectionate relative sent over from Paris once in a while were unfortunately no better—although the arrival of the first lot must have been a matter of great excitement and anticipation. Clothes from Paris! What little girl wouldn't have looked forward to trying them all on? Emily certainly did. And, of course, she found they were exquisitely made, and of beautiful materials; but they seemed much too different from what her friends wore to be comfortable, and much too childish—with their fat sashes and their delicate tucking—to be flattering. There was always at least one red dress in those trunks, too. And Emily, whose hair was a fairly violent red itself in those days (it's a nice red-gold now), felt each time that that particular frock was insult added to injury.

So, in spite of the rather extensive wardrobe she possessed, Emily's chief pleasure in those days was dressing up in her

EMILY WILKENS

EMILY WILKENS BELIEVES THAT "TEENS ARE SPECIAL PEOPLE" AND SHOULD HAVE CLOTHES "DESIGNED JUST FOR THEM." THAT'S WHAT SHE DOES, TO THE DELIGHT OF TEEN=AGERS AND THEIR MOTHERS ALIKE.

LEIGH CHARELL

THE "YOUNG BLACK" AND
FLARED SKIRT OF THIS EMILY WILKENS TEEN=AGE FROCK
ARE BECOMING TO YOUTHFUL FACES AND CAREFULLY
FASHIONED TO FLATTER YOUTHFUL FIGURES.

mother's clothes, and imagining herself already old enough to wear things that were really fashionable. In front of the mirror, pinned and tied into a dress several times too big for her, she tried to forget that it would be years and years before she could own such wonderful clothes for herself.

In the meantime she was working hard at school, and getting good marks, and it was a foregone conclusion in the Wilkens household that Emily would enter Smith College when she had finished high school. She was determined to study art and "something to do with clothes," but she was agreeable to the plan of completing a college course first, and then entering art school.

Or she *was* agreeable, until her high school art teacher scolded her once too often. The teacher had never been exactly flattering about Emily's drawings, and had pointed out upon numerous occasions that Emily didn't seem to have the ability to make even a reasonably accurate representation of the day's subject. But on the day the class was drawing a hand, she stopped beside Emily's desk and frowned down at the sketch that had just been completed. And then she said that it didn't resemble a hand at all; it looked like a dog's paw, she said, if it looked like anything.

Emily managed not to cry until she got into the locker room, but there she gave way. *How*, she asked herself despairingly, how could she ever expect to make a career in art, if she was really as bad as the teacher seemed to think she was? She *couldn't* be that bad. She just couldn't. And then her tears dried in a wave of determination. She made up her mind that she was going to have a career anyhow; she didn't care what the teacher had said. In fact, she decided right then and there, she wouldn't even take time to go to college first. She'd go right to art school after graduation. Then she'd be able to prove more quickly how wrong her teacher was.

When she announced her intention to her family, there was a good deal of argument. Her registration at Smith had already been made, and everything was settled. She couldn't change her mind now, just for a whim, her parents pointed out. But Emily was persistent. She said it wasn't a whim. It was just that she was in a hurry.

So she sent an inquiry to Pratt Institute, and pored over the literature the school mailed her in return. Designing was what she wanted to learn, she had decided. But when she found courses listed in fashion illustration and fashion design, she didn't know the difference between the two. She thought they must both be pretty much the same thing, and there was nobody around who could explain that she was mistaken. So she chose the course in illustration, and made application for the entrance examination.

It was a difficult exam, and Emily was very worried indeed until word reached her that she had passed. After that she was almost too excited to sleep. She was still having to explain regularly to her family why she didn't want to go to college, but the Wilkens' were beginning to realize that her determination was not easily broken down.

Unfortunately, just before the date of entrance, Emily became ill. She was still in bed on the day that Pratt opened for the season, and by the time she was well again, it was too late to enter that year. If Emily's ambition had been a fleeting thing, it would certainly have disappeared then. But it wasn't. Resolutely she took courses at the Hartford Art School for the rest of the season, and did so well that, when she finally entered Pratt the following fall, she was allowed to begin the second-year classes.

"I worked so hard at Pratt that all the other kids hated me," she remembers. "I did two problems for every one that was assigned to us, because I was in such a hurry to learn."

Her inability to copy exactly still made things difficult for her, but one of the teachers encouraged her real flair for quick sketching. And soon Emily was able to put down on paper with great ease and fluency the *feeling* of a thing, even if she still couldn't fill in the details with perfect accuracy. It proved to be a profitable skill. Advertisements frequently made use of just that sort of sketchy, impressionistic drawing, and during her second and last year at school Emily sold several things to magazines.

Her success along those lines suggested the next step to be taken after her graduation in 1938. Her roommate had taken a job as an apprentice in an advertising agency for $25 a week, and Emily could probably have found a similar job for herself. But she was still obsessed with the idea of haste, and that seemed to her too slow a method of advancement.

Fashion is our Business

By now, of course, she realized that although she hoped some day to design clothes, what she had studied in school had prepared her only to copy, or illustrate, the clothes that other people had designed. But she refused to be discouraged by that fact, and, armed with a huge portfolio of her work, began the long and heartbreaking round of magazines, stores and wholesale houses, seeking assignments to do sketches and illustrations.

Somewhat to her chagrin, they all persisted in disregarding her more careful drawings—the ones in which she had tried desperately hard for a true and detailed likeness—but they often looked long and approvingly at her quick little sketches. They liked the gaiety and youth she managed to inject into them, and several gave her orders on the spot for similar work to be used in ads. Emily gritted her teeth and decided to accept the orders, and forget their attitude toward the rest of her work.

Soon she was doing one sketch a week for the King Feature Syndicate, illustrations for the ads of Jane Engel, Macy's, Lord & Taylor and other New York stores; and illustrations of young people's clothes for such magazines as *The New Yorker* and *Mademoiselle*.

Her drawings were popular with the public, and made people want to own the dresses she had pictured. But the clerks and buyers in the stores weren't always so satisfied. Emily was not only inaccurate, they complained; she was sometimes downright wrong. And they would point out

that in one sketch—it was a pretty sketch, they admitted—
she had given a quite incorrect impression of the dress she'd
been supposedly copying. It was so inaccurate, they added,
that when customers came in to buy the dress they'd seen
illustrated, they were disappointed because it didn't look the
way they had thought it would.

Emily pointed out meekly that she had thought it would
look nicer the way she drew it. And the buyers suggested
acidly that if that was the way she felt—if she thought her
own ideas were so excellent—why didn't she design dresses
instead of drawing them?

Emily thought it over. Designing dresses was what she had
always wanted to do, of course. But she had these sketching
jobs right at hand. There were a good many of them now,
and she was making a very satisfactory income for one so
recently out of school. It would seem a little foolish to
abandon it all. Still—the customers who came looking for
"her" dresses had *liked* them. Maybe—

She had put the tempting thought out of her mind when
something else occurred to give her confidence in her ability
to create rather than copy, and to anticipate styles. She was
filling a sketch order one time and, on impulse, put little
aprons on the children in her drawing. It had just suddenly
occurred to her that children looked pretty in aprons. But
her employer objected, and Emily was scolded. And then,
not long afterward, pinafores for children became tremendously popular.

FASHION IS OUR BUSINESS

Emily thought that over too. She was, furthermore, beginning to feel that her free-lance work was not the most agreeable sort of work in the world. She had enough orders, it was true; she had almost too many. She found herself working all night too often, to fill them, and being cheated out of any sort of life of her own by the demands upon her time. She wasn't doing anything *but* work, she realized.

When she reached that point in her discussion with herself, she decided she wouldn't be feeling so discouraged and disgruntled if she weren't so tired. That's what was the matter with her, she told herself. She was just exhausted. And it was difficult to plan what to do with your life when you were worn out.

At that very moment a group of her friends who were on their way to California urged Emily to join them. And, on the instant, she agreed. Perhaps a rest was just what she needed. Perhaps when she came back she would be ready to work all night again; or, perhaps, she would have made up her mind to try to find a place for herself where the "different" qualities in her drawings would be considered assets rather than liabilities. In either case, the vacation would have benefited her. She had been working hard in school for three years, and working hard at her drawings for two more.

So she went off across the country and tried to forget all about art. She enjoyed herself, she swam, spent long lazy hours sunning herself, and met a lot of new friends at gay parties.

And it was—strangely enough, for a girl who had concentrated so hard on her work for so long—at one of those parties that something happened which was to influence her career dramatically. Emily was being introduced to a group of people connected with the movie industry, and the friend performing the introduction made the same mistake Emily herself had made years before. She confused fashion illustration with fashion designing—and introduced Emily as a designer.

The error didn't seem important enough to warrant correction, and when one of the guests whom she had just met asked Emily what sort of clothes she worked on, she said, "Mostly children's," and would have let it go at that. But her answer created a flurry of interest.

Ann Todd, the child actress, was about to appear in a new picture, she was informed. Why didn't she, Emily, submit sketches for her wardrobe?

Emily stared for a moment, and then she smiled. She said she would. And she added to herself that it would offer a fine opportunity to put into practice a lot of those ideas she had been frowned upon for at home.

The sketches were a success. The director liked them, and so did Ann Todd. The little actress was especially pleased because Emily talked to her very seriously, to find out just what sort of things she wanted to wear, and what sort of clothes would best express Ann's personality. And then she sketched a whole series of ensembles—not just dresses, but coats to go with them, and hats and bags and gloves that matched—and put all the sketches into a beautiful scrapbook with Ann's name on the cover. Ann could use it, Emily explained, as a sort of clothes diary.

As it turned out, that particular movie was never released. But it served its purpose in Emily's career, even so. Other youngsters saw Ann's book, and the drawings for her costumes, and begged their mothers to ask Emily to design clothes for them. Soon she was making a group of similar sketches, and similar books, for Joan Bennett's daughter, Melinda Markey; for Sandra Burns, the adopted daughter of Gracie Allen and George Burns; for Joan Benny, daughter of Mary Livingston and Jack Benny; and for other young people of the Hollywood colony. And she hired a woman to make the dresses up.

The children loved their clothes diaries, and recorded in them the parties to which they wore their new party dresses, and the various good times they had had in their new play clothes. And their mothers appreciated, as they did themselves, a designer who took youthful personalities with as much seriousness as any couturier ever lavished upon one of the world's best-dressed women.

When the Hollywood Guild wanted to stage a charity affair, it recognized the furor Emily's things had created in the community, and presented a fashion show in which Ann, Melinda, Joan, Sandra and others of Emily's clients served as models, showing their newest and favorite clothes. Melinda

Markey paraded in a Scotch plaid wool frock, with a suede jerkin, green gloves lined with the plaid and a tam trimmed with plaid; and her dog accompanied her in a plaid dog blanket. Ann Todd wore a green wool jumper with a blouse of the printed silk that was also used for the facing of a matching bonnet. Joan Benny beamed in her pale pink out-of-doors outfit, trimmed with narrow bands of fur at the collar and on the hat and muff and tiny spats. And Sandra Burns, with her hair piled on top of her head, walked serenely down the aisle in a luscious housecoat.

The affair was a tremendous success. Mothers and fathers, whose faces were familiar to thousands on the screen, smiled fondly as the guests applauded their youngsters. And the newspapers and movie magazines took wide notice of such a distinguished gathering, in stories which referred flatteringly to Emily as "The Moppets' Schiaparelli."

Emily was still so young herself—she was barely twenty-two—that it was all very exciting. Unfortunately, however, it wasn't, she soon realized, very good business. She had originally hired one woman to make up her clothes, and then she had had to hire two more. But her lack of practical experience led her into quoting prices which eventually proved too small to cover the expenses of such an establishment. There was more to making clothes, she had discovered, than merely sketching them. She was actually losing money.

She knew that she might be able to put her new business on a more practical footing, if she tried hard enough; but she didn't believe that she was basically a very good business-woman. And, besides, she had recently—since the appearance of all those stories about the fashion show—been receiving letters from stores in New York suggesting that they might be interested in sponsoring Emily's designs. So finally she decided that it was time to go home, and undertake her career there, where somebody else could handle the business details.

But that, too, proved more difficult than she had antici-pated. The war in Europe had begun, and stores had grown wary overnight of startling new ideas—even ones they had conceived of themselves. They were still interested in Emily, but they were reluctant to have her things made up them-selves. They suggested that if Emily had them made, they might consider selling them.

So she started out once more with her portfolio, and one of the first places she visited was the business office of Ben and Roy Chalk, manufacturers of junior-size coats, and of clothes for chubby girls. Roy liked the drawings, but Ben took one look at them and laughed. He admits that now, although he is today head of the wholesale house which makes up all of Emily's designs.

"One of the things *that* proves," Emily explains, "is the importance of the presentation of one's work. If I'd been able to show him real, finished models, instead of sketches, he might have taken them more seriously. But it's too easy to laugh at sketches."

These reactions—there were others like Mr. Chalk's—

weren't very pleasant to a girl who had been so widely pub-
licized in Hollywood, and who might well have come to
feel that she was already a success. But Emily didn't give up
any more easily than she had the day the teacher said her
drawing of a hand resembled a dog's paw. She continued
to make the rounds, and finally she found a manufacturer of
children's clothes who agreed to work from her designs.

The manufacturer did well with his new Wilkens originals, and they were widely sold. "But all I got out of it was
a nervous breakdown," Emily says. She adds that she realizes
now that she was too ambitious for one who couldn't sew
or drape, and that if she had been able to do those things
she might not have been regarded as so unimportant. But
since her only contribution was sketches, she wasn't given
very much credit.

Eventually she transferred to the staff of a junior clothes
manufacturer, where she designed for two years, developing
a whole line of play clothes to take the place of the evening
clothes the house had been making. Once again, it was a
profitable venture—for everybody but Emily. Saks of New
York advertised her clothes conspicuously, and fashion shows
featured them, but she wasn't satisfied.

The principal cause of her unhappiness, she finally realized,
lay in the fact that she wasn't being allowed to do the sort
of clothes she more and more wanted to do: clothes for the
teen-age girl. She had tried to suggest that the existing patterns of clothes for girls of twelve to fifteen weren't quite

right; that they didn't make proper allowance for the fact that the wearers were likely to be a little too big around the waist to fit into the standard 10-16 dresses, and that their hips were likely to be too large and their shoulders too narrow for those clothes. Their youthful figures had very special difficulties of their own—but manufacturers were going right on making dresses for them in a long-established series of standard sizes. Emily believed that not only did few girls fit into those sizes, but that they deserved special designs contrived to minimize their figure faults.

Roy and Ben Chalk had been her friends for some time now, and one day she went back to see them again. She told them exactly what she wanted to do: design exclusively for teen-age girls, with a whole new set of carefully-measured patterns that fit girls as they *were*, not as they were supposed to be; and in styles that were neither the childish styles of children's clothes, nor the too-grown-up and improperly-proportioned junior-miss sizes.

Ben Chalk was more sympathetic this time. He still felt that his own business had no room for the sort of thing Emily wanted to do, but he had become impressed with her seriousness and her determination. He thought somebody ought to give her a chance. So he arranged a meeting at which Emily could present her ideas to ten of the outstanding manufacturers of clothes for girls.

When she had completed her presentation, six of them announced flatly that they weren't interested. They were having no trouble selling the kind of clothes they were already making, they pointed out; why, they asked, should they go to all the trouble and expense of a new line?—especially in the autumn of 1943 when the restrictions of the war had made the problem of obtaining fabrics quite enough for a manufacturer to worry about. The other four all inquired cautiously what salary Emily would expect, and she said $5,000 a year. And at that they too said they weren't interested.

His generous plan a failure, Ben Chalk announced that he had changed his mind. *He* would make Emily Wilkens clothes. And without any further fuss, he inaugurated a brand new company which they called "Young Originals"— and gave Emily a free hand. She interviewed the Everfast fabric house, and managed to secure a little material. She talked to Bonwit-Teller and that New York store agreed to promote her dresses. And then she went to work.

The first collection of Emily Wilkens fashions for teen-age girls was greeted with enthusiasm by the press—all the New York papers sent their fashion writers to cover it— and with more than enthusiasm by the girls for whom the clothes had been designed, and by their mothers as well. Emily had, first of all, made her clothes according to her newly-worked-out measurements, and she gave many of them, in addition, adjustable waistlines to take care of that teen-age problem of "I seem to be a lot fatter this week than I was last." She also put gay little "wings" on shoulders, to cut down too-wide hips; and made skirts full to shrink both waists and hips. She put subtle fullness in a bodice, to suggest curves where no curves existed, or to minimize those that needed minimizing. And she gave the most careful and sympathetic attention to styles.

It was that last, of course, that endeared her things to the girls. They didn't quite know why Emily Wilkens dresses improved their figures; they didn't always appreciate the skill in the cut and fit that made them look better-proportioned than they had ever looked before. But they were perfectly aware of all the tricks of style that she offered them.

She gave them "young black," for one thing. Girls are always eager to get into their first black dress, and they frequently find their mothers reacting with a firm negative when they suggest it. But Emily Wilkens had shown them a way out of this dilemma. She made black dresses with such gay bright accessories that even the most anti-black mother couldn't feel they made her daughter look too old for her age. And the girls loved the accessories as much as they did the adultly-simple black dress with which they were worn. Emily also knew about the smallness of most allowances, and she made her things inexpensive and wonderful for shifting-around; so that girls discovered they could have three of these accessory-costumes for only slightly more than the price of one.

A popular trick for her black dress with a carefully fitted waist, a full skirt and short sleeves, was a colorful cotton bodice—low, square-necked and laced up the front. Such a bodice was not only fun to wear, but it was a special boon to the fatter-this-week-than-last girls.

Emily used the charming clothes of the 1870's as the basis for her first collection (there were rose chambray pinafores with eyelet shoulder wings and rows of tucks at the hem; and pink-and-white princess frocks with flattering back fullness), and that is a good indication of how she designs in general. She is, she says, an inveterate user of the museums of costume art and the art collections, and she doesn't see how anybody can design without knowing them well. While she was still in school she made a careful series of drawings illustrating the history of costume, and she has often and gratefully returned to them for inspiration since.

Her only other source of ideas is the teen-age girl herself. Emily is still young enough to remember how it feels to be that age, and it's easy for her to think of the sort of dresses she herself would have liked to wear then. In other words, she doesn't design down to her clients. She gives them the benefit of all her experience and all her ability, and she designs things which bring out everything that is gayest and prettiest in youthful personalities. Now her clothes are shown in the most popular fashion magazines and they are available in shops all over the country. Emily frequently visits one or another of the stores where they are sold, to watch the girls who buy them, and to keep in close touch with what girls like best in various parts of the country.

Fashion is our Business

"Teens are special people," Emily says, summing up her philosophy, "and they should have special fashions designed just for them . . . not warmed-over last year grown-up fashions, but clothes designed with the sophistication of their big sisters', cut to fit their own growing teen figures." And that is just what she makes.

Consequently the place she has, with such stubborn perseverance, made for herself in the designing profession—where she is regarded with admiration and respect by men and women old enough to be her parents—is no more secure than the place she has won in the hearts of the girls who wear her clothes. Emily Wilkens is *their* designer, and they love her for it.

FOUR

HATTIE CARNEGIE

If Hattie Carnegie is ever presented as an after-dinner speaker—which is most unlikely indeed, because that isn't the sort of thing she would enjoy, and what she doesn't enjoy she carefully avoids—the chairman would undoubtedly be tempted to resurrect that oldest and most banal of ceremonial remarks: "The speaker whom I introduce to you now really needs no introduction."

Trite or not, it would certainly be true. It is difficult to imagine that there is a woman in the United States who hasn't heard of Hattie Carnegie; and I suspect there are few men to whom her name doesn't bring to mind at least some vague thought of clothes—expensive clothes.

As a matter of fact, the aura of fame that surrounds her name has resulted in some rather strange attitudes toward Miss Carnegie herself. It has been claimed that she doesn't really exist at all as a person—that she is merely a name on a letterhead; or that she exists but doesn't—no one person *could*, some people insist—operate in any literal sense the various enterprises with which her name has been connected; that she is, in other words, merely a sort of figurehead, standing prettily but unimportantly in front of a group of businessmen who are the true managers of the business.

Fashion is our business

But Hattie Carnegie is a very real person, and a very real force in all the aspects of her many-headed organization. That fact is even more remarkable when the number and variety of those aspects is made clear. At present they include, besides a retail shop at Palm Beach, three large establishments in New York City.

There is, first of all, the elaborate retail and custom shop —almost a department store in size and scope—at 42 East 49th Street, in the center of the city's most fashionable buying district. Here, on the second floor of the block-through building, is the gilt-and-mirrored custom salon—its furnishings were all imported from Paris—where models parade twice a day in Hattie Carnegie originals. Wealthy customers may purchase custom-made copies of these gowns for from $250 to $500.

On the same floor is the fur salon, where Carnegie-designed fur coats and wraps are shown; the comparatively new antique shop—an expression of Miss Carnegie's own eager interest in lovely old furniture, glass and china; and a section where Carnegie chocolates, the most recent product to bear her name, are sold.

On the ground floor of the building are several subsidiary departments. There is the bag shop, where Miss Carnegie's own bag designs are sold; the jewelry department; the cosmetic and perfume department (Carnegie cosmetics and perfumes are also sold throughout the country); the blouse and sweater department; a ready-to-wear hat shop, with models

PHYFE

ΗΑΤΤΙΕ CARNEGIE

HATTIE CARNEGIE'S FORCEFUL PER=
SONALITY AND UNERRING KNOWLEDGE OF WHAT MAKES
A DRESS "GOOD" ARE THE FOUNDATIONS OF HER WIDE
REPUTATION AND HER REMARKABLE BUSINESS SUCCESS.

LARRY GORDON

HATTIE CARNEGIE FASHIONS LAVISH MATERIALS INTO "LITTLE DRESSES" OR "LITTLE SUITS"—LIKE THE ABOVE—SO CONSERVATIVELY RIGHT THAT THEY PLAY UP, RATHER THAN DOMINATE, A WOMAN'S PERSONALITY.

that sell for from $5 to $25; and the custom hat shop where copies of original numbers bring from $30 to $65; a ready-to-wear dress department, where copies of Carnegie originals made up in standard sizes may be purchased for as little as $110, together with gowns by other designers carefully selected for this shop by Miss Carnegie's buyers; a second ready-to-wear department, known as the Jeune Fille Shop, where inexpensive garments (under $50, that is) include Carnegie models from her own Spectator Sports wholesale house, and a variety of models from other houses; and, finally, the hostess pajama and underwear department, where many of the pajama models are Miss Carnegie's own.

Between Thanksgiving and Christmas of every year there is added to this array the Carnegie Blue Room for Men, a comfortable corner where floundering, gift-seeking males are advised and guided in their purchases by expert saleswomen.

The upper three floors of this building are used for workrooms, and it is there that Carnegie custom designs are originated, and the custom orders are filled.

Several blocks away, at 711 Fifth Avenue, are the Carnegie wholesale workrooms and salon. There copies of Carnegie originals are made up in standard sizes, and shown to buyers—they represent a selected group of stores throughout the country, and never more than one to each city—who come to New York to choose the models they wish to feature.

And then—yes, there is still one more establishment—at 530 Seventh Avenue is the Spectator Sports wholesale house.

FASHION IS OUR BUSINESS

There are less expensive dresses, suits and coats—their prices range from $29.50 to $98.50 wholesale—are designed to supply the East 49th Street shop, and another and larger group of buyers from various shops in the forty-eight states, who come here to make purchases.

If you'd think such an astounding array of business ventures would get out of hand; if you'd hardly believe one woman could keep her eye on all of them at once—you don't know Miss Carnegie, that's all. It is true that she does display a certain apparent vagueness in regard to her various enterprises, but hard-headed business men agree that the vagueness can only be pretended. Amusing proof of the soundness of their judgment may be found in the reports of various Carnegie saleswomen. They declare that Miss Carnegie often smiles at a customer, and murmurs, "My dear, how pretty you look in that dress. Where did you get it?" Whereupon the customer, somewhat surprised, explains that she bought it from Miss Carnegie the previous season. "Dear me," Miss Carnegie always says then, looking pleased, "I must have forgotten." But never, the saleswomen claim, have they ever heard her make such a comment about a dress which wasn't purchased from her own collection.

Her story is remarkable when it is viewed from the beginning. Hattie—she was christened Henrietta Kanengeiser—was born in Vienna in 1889, the second eldest of seven children. Things were never very easy for the family and, when their house burned down, Mr. Kanengeiser decided to come to

America where there might be better opportunities for making a good living for his family. He crossed the Atlantic alone, and gradually sent back money to allow his wife and children to follow him.

Legend has it that the little Henrietta—she was already called Hattie, for short—inquired on shipboard as to who was the richest and most famous man in America. An indulgent steward, smiling down at her, said he supposed Andrew Carnegie might be called that. And at that moment, the story runs, Hattie made up her mind to adopt that name for herself, as a sort of good-luck talisman.

Whatever the real reason—perhaps Carnegie was simply easier to spell, and a natural Americanization of their Austrian name—the family which settled down on St. Marks Place, in lower New York, became known among their neighbors as the Carnegies. Hattie went to a public school until, in her early teens, she saw an advertisement for an assistant in a millinery workroom, and she went to work pinning up hats. She hasn't stopped working since.

There followed a series of various jobs—once she was a runner in Macy's—all of which served to initiate her into the inner workings of manufacturing and selling women's wear. And, in 1909, she and a friend of hers, Rose Roth, opened a tiny hat and dress shop of their own on East Tenth Street. It was called "Carnegie—Ladies' Hatter."

Rose was a seamstress, and it was she who made the dresses. Hattie doesn't sew herself, and never could, so she made hats and waited on customers. It was a modest place, but their prices weren't in the least modest. And their customers, hoping they themselves would look as chic in the things they bought as Hattie herself did, were willing enough to pay the sums they were asked.

Even then Miss Carnegie was showing clear evidence of the exquisite good taste which is and always has been the very foundation of her business. Even if she couldn't stitch a dress together, she could tell in an instant whether a certain frock was "good" or not, and—if it wasn't—what it needed to improve it. It may have been true that early customers, not, perhaps, endowed with Hattie's own tiny figure and her indefinable air of smartness, didn't look so well as Hattie did in the frocks they bought; but they usually did look better than they ever had before. And so they came back again and again to the small shop and "Carnegie—Ladies' Hatter" became a financial success. By 1913 the two young owners were able to incorporate with a capital of $100,000, and open a new shop on West Eighty-Sixth Street.

They chose the location because it was near the then-fashionable Riverside Drive. It was, unfortunately, wedged between a delicatessen shop and a Chinese restaurant, but the wealthy customers they were hoping for sought them out in spite of the numerous odors wafted into the fitting rooms. In those days fashionable women looked instinctively, not to large stores, but to "little dressmakers" for their clothes, and the Carnegie models were "discovered" by one smart woman after another.

Hattie's confidence in herself grew. She watched the Paris styles with a sharp eye, and adapted them with unerring success for American women. She never, even then, claimed to be a pioneer in the introduction of new and different lines and silhouettes; but she could choose from the season's innovations those which would make her customers look their prettiest. And, though she could not even sketch her ideas on paper, much less cut and drape them into actual shape, she could always make clear to her workers what she wanted done—and criticize and encourage and prod until she had the exact results she desired.

Finally she bought out her partner and, as Hattie Carnegie, Inc., launched the one-woman business that has grown so astoundingly ever since. By 1919 she felt she could afford a trip abroad, and she rushed over to Paris to see at first-hand the most fashionable women in the world and the salons where they were dressed. She had loved Paris before she had ever seen it, and she has always loved it. But she never allowed it to sway her from her own opinions and her own sense of what was right; so, although she brought back with her, and sold, copies of the newest and latest models from the showrooms of Vionnet and Chanel and the other great French houses, she always also made up her own adaptations of their designs. And many American women came to feel that they were more likely to be satisfied with a dress if it was a Carnegie model, than if it were an exact duplicate of a striking novelty just launched on the Rue de la Paix.

In 1926 Miss Carnegie discovered—rather to her surprise, of course—that she had a sizable sum on hand, and she bought the building on East 49th Street which, together with the building next door, purchased later, is still her headquarters.

The economic crisis of 1929 didn't affect Miss Carnegie at first. She was doing beautifully herself—three-and-a-half million dollars' worth of clothes a year sounded to her like a pretty good business for a young immigrant girl to have built up for herself—but suddenly she noticed that her customers weren't able to pay their bills. Sometimes the customers didn't realize their own predicament right away, and went on ordering dresses that cost as much as seven hundred dollars, and ten-dollar handkerchiefs—only to report tearfully later on that their husbands had been ruined in the stock market crash, and they couldn't pay.

The Carnegie business had been a luxury business from the start, but once Miss Carnegie came out of her "vagueness" to a full realization of the trend of the times, she reacted with characteristic speed. She opened that ready-to-wear department on the ground floor of her shop, for inexpensive clothes, and she took the additional and far more drastic—for her—step of inaugurating the Spectator Sports establishment, to manufacture clothes which could sell for as low as $26.50. She had been dealing in high-priced garments for so long that she was actually surprised to discover that dresses could be made to sell at that price. And she was further surprised to find that the new Spectator Sports line, sold throughout the country, began to bring her in a larger income than she had ever made from her high-priced clothes.

Her shift from a purely custom business to one including a ready-to-wear line was symptomatic of the times. Miss Carnegie had been an outstanding source, in America, of all that was best—and most expensive—from the Paris houses. Now, with American women of all economic levels being aware of and wanting good clothes at reasonable prices, she became a leader in the manufacture of ready-to-wear clothes on a large scale. Of course she didn't give up the custom section of her business, and gradually it climbed back toward its pre-1929 status. And Miss Carnegie calmly settled down to manage two divergent types of enterprise, as nonchalantly as if they were two customers wanting slightly different kinds of dresses.

Her brother, Herman Carnegie, became her secretary and treasurer, and as time went on she took several other members of her family and several friends into the rapidly growing ranks of her employes. She has always hired people for the same reason that she chooses one particular kind of collar from several possibilities: as a matter of personal and intimate choice. She always knows instantly whom and what she likes. She keeps her employes, many of them, for years on end, and treats them with mingled warmth and sternness, shot through with exhibitions of her lightning-flash temper.

Fashion is our Business

Once, the story runs,[*] she came upon two idle girls in the workroom, and suddenly flared into such a furious tirade against their laziness that they were both reduced to tears. Whereupon Miss Carnegie marched away, only to return a few moments later to thrust a comforting handkerchief at them—and to murmur, "And furthermore, crying on my time!"

She is just as ready to loan one of her salesgirls an elaborate Carnegie model for an important date, as she is to scold her for a trivial lapse. In short, she keeps her whole staff as aware of her as she herself is aware, actually, of every detail of her establishment—despite that convenient vagueness which permits her to overlook anything she doesn't want to concern herself with. But let an employe think to take advantage of that vagueness, and Miss Carnegie suddenly galvanizes into attention, and proceeds to prove that she knows everything that needs to be known about the incident at hand.

She keeps that same all-seeing eye on her collections. The two designers who work in her custom department, the other two who design in the wholesale rooms on Fifth Avenue, and the designer at the Spectator Sports establishment, are all under her constant supervision. They sketch and make up models, sometimes on their own initiative, sometimes at her suggestions; but in either case she goes over each one and orders the removal of a pocket, the changing of a neckline,

[*] "Hattie Carnegie," *Cosmopolitan*, Inez Robb, CXII, No. 6 (June 1942), p. 8.

the shifting of a waistline, to bring the garment into focus according to the standards of taste which are her stock in trade. And when a collection is nearly ready for showing, Miss Carnegie studies it as a whole, makes corrections and points out its omissions. ("There isn't a box-jacketed suit in the lot," she may discover. "We have customers who always want box jackets. Make some.")

In other words, she serves in the same capacity as does the editor of a magazine, and stamps her clothes as clearly with her personality as any editor ever stamps a publication. Just as an editor draws up a general policy for a magazine, and outlines the contents for each issue, so Hattie Carnegie establishes the policy for her clothes and indicates the types of garments she wants made up each season. And then, when the assistants have brought her their contributions, she treats them again as an editor treats the pieces of writing that come to his desk. She moves a line from here to there—as an editor may shift a paragraph from page 3 to page 4, where he believes it will be more effective; she suggests a greater emphasis on this or that; and she makes the final choice of what completed, revised piece of work is to be shown to the customers.

Her policy is that—as she once titled an article she wrote—"Fads Aren't Fashion." * In that article she discussed the period clothes which her friend and customer, Norma Shearer, was wearing in the motion picture, *Marie Antoinette*.

* *Pictorial Review*, Vol. 39, No. 12, Sept. '35, p. 21.

FASHION IS OUR BUSINESS

She described the foolishly elaborate coiffeurs—the wig with the birdcage on top, and the. wig in which tiny farm buildings, a farmer and his wife, and a whole assortment of miniature barnyard animals perched atop a froth of hair—and she described the eighty-pound ball dress which had to be hoisted over the actress's shoulders by eight girls. And then she wrote:

"The preview of the picture set me to thinking of women's clothes through the ages. Fashions come and go, changing endlessly, borrowing from the past, creating for the future, repeating, rearranging . . . with Norma Shearer I say that women today *are* lucky. We can dress simply, with quiet, classic care for line, color, and the natural contours of the body. We can be natural and unaffected. Of course we must in all fairness admit that we are addicted to *some* follies. A Frenchman who lived during Marie Antoinette's reign wrote: 'Never before have French women spent so much money simply to make themselves ridiculous.' Today our husbands and beaus say the same thing about *us* when they see some of our hats.

"I like silly hats, myself. I think that a hat can be frivolous, full of flowers or fruits or quaint veiling, and that even the gentlemen won't object, if it is becoming. It's not gay, silly fashions which men really dislike. It's clothes that don't flatter and suit you that make them say: 'Why *do* you women have to wear such crazy hats?' Or dresses, or shoes, as the case may be. If you never buy anything simply because it's

64

amusing or smart or new, but wear only the clothes that make *you* amusing, *you* smart, *you* new, you'll be the envy of all the women you know, the admiration of all the men."

And then she quotes from a letter written to the real Marie Antoinette by her sober Austrian mother, Maria Theresa. "Dear Toinette," the letter ran, "you know I have always held that it is well to be in the fashion to a reasonable extent, but that one should never be *outre* in one's dress."

"Let her guide you in choosing clothes, too," Miss Carnegie concludes. "Once more let me underscore her sage advice: *'Be in the fashion to a reasonable extent'*—but remember that your own personality and charms are of primary importance, and that the simplest, neatest clothes set these off to best advantage."

As a designer and a saleswoman for her own clothes, Miss Carnegie gives that advice to her customers as she gave it to the readers of that article. Her adaptations of "new" styles have always been made with one eye on the style itself, and one on the American woman who is to wear it. If one of her favorite French designers introduces a brand new waistline which Miss Carnegie doesn't think will be becoming to American women, or comfortable for them to wear, she ignores it as if it were a plague.

One incident, which may seem to contradict that fact, actually serves as its most striking example. Just before the war she returned from one of her buying trips to Europe with a corset which a Parisian house had introduced as the basis of its new and startling silhouette. Miss Carnegie had bought the corset, and intended to use it—and the line it created—in her own forthcoming collection. American designers watched her with eager interest, as they always do. Miss Carnegie had made a fortune for herself by giving American women what they wanted—what made them "prettier." Would her customers accept this, after so many years of corsetless freedom, just because they had come to accept Miss Carnegie's advice more or less automatically?

But before her collection could be put to the test, in a showing for her customers, she wore one of the corsets herself on a plane trip West, to attend an important fashion showing at which she was to be a guest of honor. Before the plane had completed a half-hour of its long jaunt, Miss Carnegie began to look very uncomfortable indeed. She couldn't breathe very well and she was beginning to feel ill. And a few moments later she made one of the quick decisions which is so characteristic of her. She disappeared into the dressing room, rang for her secretary and for the stewardess, and, at her orders, they tugged and pulled until they had removed the Carnegie corset from the Carnegie figure. Miss Carnegie then took a deep breath, glared at the offending garment, remarked that it was not so much a corset as a casket—and consigned it to oblivion on the spot. And she did it without a second's qualm over the fact that she knew reporters would be waiting at the airport to witness her arrival in the corset already so famous that its reputation had preceded it across the continent.

She never suggests to a customer that the customer wear something so startling that Miss Carnegie wouldn't wear it herself. And she never wears startling clothes. The "little black dress" for which she is so well-known, the dress that is "right" everywhere and at almost any time, is typical of the clothes for which her customers are most grateful. She likes suits, and makes them up for every hour of the day and evening. She uses beautiful, lavish materials, but uses them in such a way that the woman wearing them is never overshadowed by their magnificence. And she likes to "orchestrate" a costume, believing that a "well-groomed woman should be as perfectly coordinated as a well-turned-out piece of music."

Before the war, and the minute Paris was freed again, French designers watched Miss Carnegie's reactions to their collections with a careful eye. They knew that what she took back to America with her was a good indication of what they might expect to sell most successfully to the American women who bought from them directly, and to the other buyers who visited their showing and who also watched Miss Carnegie's choices. And the wholesalers on Seventh Avenue keep accurate account of what she is introducing, because they know they can profitably follow her trends.

Miss Carnegie rules her household as competently as she rules her business, and her husband—Major John Zanft—

thinks she is the most wonderful woman in the world. So do dozens of her customers, including some of the best-dressed women in the country. Many of them insist upon her personal advice and buy whatever she tells them to buy. Gertrude Lawrence, the actress, not only wears Carnegie clothes in her off-stage life, but had Miss Carnegie design all the beautiful things she wore in the stage production of *Lady in the Dark*. Other actresses whom the designer has dressed both off-stage and on include Elisabeth Bergner, Ina Claire, Ruth Gordon, Joan Crawford, Joan Fontaine and Margaret Sullavan.

Her customers trust her. They may object to her prices, but they know that there is a reason for them—that Carnegie clothes are fashioned with an attention to detail which makers of inexpensive clothes cannot afford. And they know, too, that Hattie Carnegie loves clothes—good clothes—and won't sell anything that she doesn't honestly think is good. To Miss Carnegie a dress that isn't *very* good, is very, very bad. And when a thing looks bad to Miss Carnegie, she assumes without question that it will look that way to countless other women. The enormous size of her clientele proves that she is right about that, as she is about most things.

FIVE

CLAIRE McCARDELL

Fashion writers searching for a phrase to describe Claire McCardell almost inevitably settle upon one that begins with the words "as American as . . ." She has been called "as American as mince pie," "as American as the Fourth of July," and "as American as a village store." And, with less originality perhaps, but just as pointedly, she has been referred to over and over again simply as "typically American."

In 1941, *Vogue*, writing about this already-outstanding young designer, said she represented exactly the sort of person Europeans had in mind when, newly arrived in this country, they said they were "most impressed with your beautiful tall buildings and your beautiful American girls."

"She looks exactly like . . . The Typical American Girl —whom you never saw, but read about in print," *Vogue* said. "There she is, working over on Seventh Avenue, sprung full-panoplied from the newspaper type, and looking just as real as real. Only prettier. She's glowing with health—her tanned skin shines with it. Her face is made flippant by a tilted nose, enthusiastic eyes. Her figure is long and lithe, her legs are long and lovely. And she's young, fresh, perfectly turned out, full of slang and laughs."

Vogue has said it about as well as anybody can—though it

might have mentioned in addition the characteristic way Claire does her hair, rolling it up, catching it into a net, and fastening it with whatever tiny flowers or huge pins have most recently caught her fancy. But you didn't need that description if you know Claire McCardell's clothes. And it's likely you do, since they have been widely advertised by name for some time. For she and the dresses she designs are very much alike—easy and casual, sensible and workmanlike and gay, all at once.

Claire not only looks and acts the part of a "typical American." She grew up according to a formula that fits that phrase. She is a small-town girl who triumphed over early failures to make good in the big city, for all the world like a feminine counterpart of an Alger hero.

Born in Frederick, Maryland, Claire spent her childhood there in a comfortable, pretty house with her parents and her three younger brothers. She helped with the housework, went to school, played with the neighborhood children, and cut out paper dolls. It was her attitude toward the paper dolls that gave the closest hint of what her future was to be.

She loved them, and spent long hours over them. But she only liked a very special kind. The curly-headed little-girl dolls that were sold in the stores didn't interest her at all. She made her own, grown-up and elegant, from the fashion magazines her mother bought. And she says she can remember waiting impatiently for Mrs. McCardell to finish with the new issues and turn them over to her. Claire's special

CLAIRE McCARDELL

"TYPICALLY AMERICAN," CLAIRE McCARDELL'S CLOTHES ARE SOLUTIONS TO THE VARIOUS PROBLEMS OF EVERYDAY LIVING. SHE LIKES THEM TO BE GAY AND PRETTY, BUT DEMANDS FIRST OF ALL, THAT THEY WORK.

LOUISA DAHL-WOLFE, COURTESY HARPER'S BAZAAR

A STURDY MATERIAL, A WEALTH OF CONVENIENT POCKETS, A CUT THAT COMBINES COMFORT AND YOUTHFUL SMARTNESS, MAKE THIS SPORTS COSTUME REPRESENTATIVE OF CLAIRE McCARDELL'S FASHION PHILOSOPHY.

pleasure was to dress her lovely glossy-paper ladies in clothes properly suited to various activities—dinner parties, teas and dances.

Probably there are little girls all over the country who do that today, and doubtless many of the creatures they snip from the magazine pages are wearing dresses that Claire has designed. But those dresses are very different from the ones Claire used to cut out herself. And in that difference lies the story of her growing-up, and of the influence she has had on American clothes. Because Claire discovered over the years that very few people spend their lives, as had her dolls, in gleaming ballrooms and exquisitely-furnished drawing rooms. They're much more likely to be working in an office, or keeping house, or studying in chilly college dormitories. And so, though her designs today are like her paper-doll dresses in that they are suited to particular occasions, the occasions have vastly changed. Claire has learned a lot since she first took the scissors to her mother's magazines, and she uses every bit of her knowledge and experience in her work.

The apprenticeship of the paper dolls was, however, a valuable first step. She says, "My fingers cut the silhouette of the moment, and my eyes began their training."

There were other steps, too, that she took while she was still small. Like most children, she "played lady," in her mother's clothes, fastening long skirts up with pins and posing in front of the mirror in imitation of the studiously graceful models she so admired. Her brothers made fun of her sometimes, but when Claire took off the makeshift garments and played games with the boys, they had to admit that she wasn't a sissy. She liked sports, she liked to do active things in general.

Of course it didn't occur to them, and it didn't occur to Claire then either, that the hours she spent at games were also giving her necessary background and training. In front of the mirror she could learn what was becoming, but playing with her brothers taught her that some clothes, pretty though they might be, just got in the way when one was climbing a tree or leading the hunt in Run, Sheep, Run. Both kinds of knowledge were useful to her future career.

Even then, she says, she knew vaguely what that career was to be. She knew, at least, that it would have something to do with clothes. So when Miss Annie came twice a year to make the family wardrobe, Claire set herself down on the opposite side of the sewing machine and watched the seamstress put things together.

Eventually she tried her hand at sewing herself. "But I was always in such a hurry to try my creations on that I didn't have the patience to make them carefully," she says with a reminiscent grin. "I didn't sew very well, but I managed to get an 'effect,' you might say."

Her first ventures were all at remodeling. And later on, when she had graduated to the making of new dresses out of cloth purchased especially for the purpose, she went right on making things over. Because, as she put it, changing things around was so much fun. She tried everything—coats and suits and hats and even masquerade costumes, in addition to ordinary dresses for school and Sunday wear. Everything interested her, at least for a while, and she loved to experiment. Her fingers were more than usually clever at achieving that "effect" she wanted, but she was doubtless scolded a good many times by her mother and by Miss Annie for that restless impatience of hers.

When she was through high school Claire entered Hood College, in her home town, and life went on pretty much as it had before. Unfortunately, however, according to her point of view, Hood wouldn't allow its students to take sewing courses and nothing else. The curriculum provided for sciences too, and other such difficult subjects. Claire didn't like them.

"My chemistry professor told me that the only thing I really learned in his course was that acid can burn the human skin," she says. "The blisters on my hands were proof that I had permanently memorized that one fact."

Reasonably enough, the professor didn't seem to think that amount of information was sufficient. Gradually he and a few other teachers, and finally Claire's parents and Claire herself, came to the conclusion that she would do better in an art school.

So, at the end of her sophomore year, she came to New York and—as so many potential designers had done before her—entered the Parsons School. The new life was wonderful and exciting. It wasn't only that every one of her classes interested her. There was the additional joy of living at the Three Arts Club, where she became acquainted with a wide group of girls whose interests were similar to hers and who, like Claire, were eagerly tasting the freedom of being on their own and the satisfaction of studying the things they most wanted to learn.

Furthermore, the club owned a wardrobe of old costumes for the girls' use in plays and masquerades. Claire's first sight of it was like an explorer's glimpse of a brand new island. Here was a wonderful opportunity to make things over to her heart's content. Claire ripped and pinned and basted with enthusiasm, unhampered by the shadow of Miss Annie standing at her shoulder to say sternly that a good effect wasn't enough. An effect *was* all one needed for garments to be worn on the stage, and it was heaven to throw a costume together without having to concern oneself with pinking the seams and putting buttons on tightly enough to withstand hard wear.

Claire might have been fatally encouraged in her youthful contentment with results that wouldn't survive a close inspection, if it hadn't been for one more new influence that entered her life about that time. The Three Arts was sponsored by a board of directors composed of wealthy women, and one of the ways they helped their young members to stretch their allowances, was to give the club their own discarded clothes, many of them French importations. The girls were allowed to purchase these garments for as little as five dollars, and Claire was at first simply overjoyed at a new and wonderfully inexpensive opportunity to make things over —and for herself, this time.

But after she had handled those frocks for a while, and worn them, she began to notice the tiny, intricate tucking, the carefully-worked seams, and the delicate hand details. They were little things, perhaps—things that took a great deal of time and patience, but that you wouldn't see from the audience side of the footlights or even in your own mirror if you squinted your eyes slightly and concentrated your attention on the general impression. But they did, she began to realize, make a difference. They set these French clothes very far apart indeed from her own careless efforts. Claire's first taste of the exquisite art of Parisian dressmaking taught her a lesson that she didn't forget.

It also convinced her that she had to get to Paris herself, to learn more about a business which was, she now knew, far more difficult and complicated than she had recognized. So the next year she transferred to the Paris branch of the Parsons School, in the Place des Vosges.

Going abroad by herself at that age was a delicious excitement in itself. And at that time the French franc was worth only a few cents of American money, so Claire's small allowance permitted her to live in comparative luxury. She considered herself positively rich when she was able to earn a little extra money to add to her regular funds, and she did that frequently by working odd hours in an office that sold sketches of Paris models. Claire wasn't a particularly talented sketcher, but she and several of her fellow-students were hired in rush seasons to make tracings of skilled artists' drawings. That was easy enough, and instructive too; you couldn't trace the outlines of a dress innumerable times without learning something about it, and why it was being so eagerly sought after.

She also soon discovered that the Paris dress houses sold their showroom models at very low prices, when the season was over. She took advantage of that fact to acquire more beautifully-made things for herself, to wear and make over and study.

"I was learning important things all the time," she says of that year, "—the way clothes worked, the way they felt, where they fastened."

So naturally, after a third and final year back at the New York Parsons, she felt that she was fairly well-educated about clothes, and ready for a good job.

She started out light-heartedly enough, in spite of her natural shyness about meeting people. After all, hadn't she been to Paris? And it was 1928 and the world was almost giddily prosperous. But day after day, from agency to agency, she made the rounds without success. Curt businessmen had little time for bright young girls just out of school. There were too many of them. Claire wasn't much good at talking about herself, and an affectionate family and three happy years at school hadn't prepared her for constant rebuffs.

A whole long month went by, and Claire learned to eat quick, inexpensive lunches at drug store counters, to smile cheerfully when she wanted to burst into tears. And she learned too how difficult it is to keep looking fresh and well-groomed and pretty in a grimy city and on very little money. But hundreds of other girls were faced with the same problems, so Claire gritted her teeth and kept on.

At the end of the second month somebody finally hired her—to paint rosebuds on lampshades. She had pictured herself as a smart fashion artist, an illustrator—as anything but this. And though she accepted the job and went grimly to work, she couldn't stand it. "The rosebuds made me sick," she says, and so they did, quite literally—the rosebuds and the weary disappointing weeks that had preceded them. Sniffling and red-eyed and running a temperature from a heavy cold, Claire walked out, climbed on board a train and went home to Maryland.

But as soon as she got there she knew she'd made a mistake. Maybe rosebuds wasn't the right next step, but Frederick wasn't either—unless she was giving up. By the end of a week her cold was cured and her confidence was restored. She set out for New York again, determined to stick this time no matter what happened.

And this time she fared a little better. She got a job, and even if it wasn't much of a job, at least it gave her a chance to see clothes and handle them. She was a model at Altman's, in the salon where the French imports were sold. It wasn't much fun, and she says she wasn't a very good model, but she kept at it.

And then one day the Parsons School recommended her for a sketching job with Emmet Joyce, whose beautiful clothes sold for fabulously high prices. Claire was pleased, in spite of the fact that she would earn only $20 a week. Now, low salary or not, she was inside. She was actually working in a dress house.

The excellent Joyce reputation impressed others too. And a few weeks after Claire went to work there, a friend introduced her to a knit-goods manufacturer who immediately made up his mind that she must be a very gifted young woman indeed to be employed there. Without hesitation he offered her $40 a week to serve as his assistant.

Claire gulped and accepted. There were miracles, after all. Here she was, only a short time out of school, really (it was easy to make light of those months of job-hunting and the dreadful rosebuds, now that they were in the past), and already she was an assistant to the head of a wholesale house. She plunged into the new job with pride and enthusiasm.

The pride, unfortunately, proved to be a little premature. Designing knit wear was a rather specialized business. And though Claire concentrated eagerly on learning all she could about it, her employer learned something too. He discovered that Claire wasn't actually a designer, even if she had been associated with an expensive dress house. He could see she was a smart girl, and that she might amount to something some day; but what he needed right then was a trained, experienced helper, not just a bright youngster with more ideas than knowledge. So at the end of eight months he fired her.

That time the round of job-hunting was real torture. She had been so sure she was on her way—and now she was right back at the bottom again, visiting the agencies every day. Should she admit to not having much experience? Or should she say she had already had a pretty good job—and lost it?

Once again two months went by before she found something. But when she did, Claire realized that it was exactly what she needed, and that she was incredibly lucky, even if some aspects of the new job were fairly unpleasant. She was now a sort of general helper—nothing so formal as an assistant—in another wholesale house. She sketched, bought buttons and belts, ran the sample room, fitted dresses on herself and then modeled them for costumers—in short she did most of the odd jobs that needed doing in a small place. "I didn't sweep the floors," she says, "but I don't remember why. I did practically everything else."

One of the least pleasant aspects of the work, from the point of view of a still-shy Claire, was the regular trips she was expected to make through the city's better stores, picking up ideas which might be useful. She knew such trips were standard practice among dress houses, but to a Maryland conscience they pretty closely resembled spying. Anyhow, she felt as guilty as a spy could feel, walking with feigned nonchalance past a striking dress, trying desperately to memorize its details from a brief glance out of the corner of her eye, and then shutting herself into a telephone booth to sketch it hastily before she had forgotten what she saw. She hated it. And finally she discovered that it was much easier to invent new ideas of her own, and take sketches of them back to the office. Nobody ever asked her where they came from. In fact, nobody ever challenged her offerings at all.

"Maybe my boss, Robert Turk, really didn't catch on—or maybe he just liked my originals and let me alone," Miss McCardell says.

In any case he didn't fire her. And in 1931, two years after she had gone to work for him, he took her along when he was made the designer for Townley Frocks.

Claire was working hard, but she knew how valuable a training she was getting. She was learning from every angle how dresses are designed, manufactured and sold. She was learning how a business operates. Every day she realized more clearly how right the knit-goods manufacturer had been to let her go. She hadn't been a designer then at all. Now, vividly aware of the enormous complexity of the career she had chosen, she wondered if she ever would be. And then something happened.

Mr. Turk died suddenly, by drowning. At first Claire could only stare numbly, trying to comprehend the news. He had been her friend and teacher, as well as her employer. He had been so patient with her, taught her so much. And now he was gone.

The rest of the Townley staff were as shocked as she was, but they pulled themselves together in the face of the problem that now confronted them. The forthcoming collection was still unfinished, and machines and workmen would stand idle if it could not be completed in time for the regular showing. Someone must be found, and soon, to carry on Mr. Turk's work. And in the middle of a season it was unlikely that a well-known designer could be hired at short notice.

For a while Claire scarcely understood when they told her what they had decided: they wanted her to do the job herself. Now? To assume such a responsibility when—?

But the work had to be done, and any sort of work was a steadying thing. Almost automatically, and too upset to be as frightened as she might otherwise have been, Claire settled down to the task she had been given.

On the day of the showing she was too busy to know how it was being received. As her own boss and her own assistant, she was everywhere at once, fitting, draping, pinning, worrying. The models had to make their appearance in a steady procession. She could only concern herself with getting them on the floor. There was no time to wonder whether the customers out front were smiling or frowning, whether they liked what they saw, or whether they were whispering to each other behind their smartly gloved hands that of course, under the circumstances—some mere girl had had to take the collection over midway and finish it herself—things were probably no worse than you'd expect.

But the next morning she and the whole fashion world knew that the understudy had proved herself. The clothes she had sketched so frantically and in such haste, that she would have been terrified to send out into the show room if she had had time for terror, were a success.

The Townley staff breathed a sigh and relaxed. It wouldn't be necessary now to search for a new designer. They had one. Her name was Claire McCardell and they were proud of her.

Claire was proud too, but more than a little nervous. She reminded herself that the knit goods manufacturer had once thought she was a designer too, but he soon found out he had made a mistake. Would Townley discover that it too had been wrong?

So she moved carefully, feeling her way ahead. There were a lot of brand new ideas buzzing around in her mind, and sometimes, relaxing at home, she ripped up an old dress and pinned it together in a new way that delighted her. But she hesitated to take such things into the office. The head designer for a wholesale house had a serious responsibility, and she mustn't jeopardize her employer's reputation by unadvised experimentation.

Part of her new job was to go to Paris twice a year, and

the first of those trips was unalloyed pleasure. It was tremendously exciting to renew her youthful acquaintance with the city, and to appear in her professional role at the salons which she had entered only as a timid student several years earlier—and then only on "sale" days when the season's showings were over.

And besides, such trips were scarcely work at all. Claire was simply supposed to do what most American designers did: sketch the new models and bring her drawings home to be copied as accurately as possible for the American trade.

But after a while the originality that is so characteristic of her found that program limiting. She loved the Paris dresses, and she appreciated the skill and beauty with which they were made. But they didn't seem to her fully adapted to the sort of busy, active life American women and girls led. She could remember too clearly the problems of dressing attractively when you were looking for a job, or—when you had found one—of dressing on twenty dollars a week. The thousands of girls who were doing that liked pretty clothes as well as their wealthier sisters did, and they had even more need of gaiety in what they wore, because there was less of it in their lives. But they had to take care of their clothes themselves, so they didn't want trimmings that were fussy, or materials that wrinkled easily. And they liked to be comfortable, not only at their desks and benches, but later on, when they went to a movie or drove out into the country on a picnic.

"Somehow," Claire said, with those girls in mind, "I had a feeling I wanted to do a different kind of clothes than the ones I saw."

So, very cautiously at first, she attempted deviations from the sketches she brought back to New York. She followed the basic trends of each season's dictates as to line and silhouette, but, to use her own words, she translated what she saw into "American fabrics, making them a little easier, a little more casual, a little less self-conscious, and a little more American."

She was still afraid to go too far, and frequently when she had had a dress made up in the workroom according to one of her new "translations," she obeyed the warnings of her soberer second thoughts and didn't show it to customers at all. But she always wore the experiments herself (that didn't necessitate any changes; she happens to be model size), and they felt the way she had wanted them to feel.

In 1937 Claire designed an Algerian costume for herself, to wear to the Beaux Arts Ball. It was long and full, secured at the waist by a broad belt. She liked the looseness of it, and the way the material hung in soft folds. In fact it was so comfortable, and so much fun to wear, that she made up a short red wool dress for herself afterward, modeled on the same lines and held around her slim waist by a wide leather belt. Of course she wouldn't show it to customers.

She knew better than to expect buyers to take seriously anything so revolutionary and strange.

But for once Claire was too cautious. Somehow someone caught sight of that shapeless, smock-like garment and decided to take a chance on it. American women might just be ready for something so incredibly easy to wear and so refreshingly different. And they were. Almost overnight they took it to their hearts. It had no "fit" at all to worry about. It hung like a sack—until you pulled a belt around your waist and miraculously transformed a complete lack of line into a flowing symphony of lines. Here, women seemed instinctively to realize, was an American dress. Perhaps only tall, free-striding American girls could wear it, but they could wear it superbly well.

Best's, in New York, called it the "monastic dress," and other shops chose their own names. But almost all of them carried it. It swept through the entire dress market, copied and recopied, at every imaginable price. And Claire McCardell had established herself not only as a competent designer, but as a strikingly original one.

In the years that followed that sort of thing was to happen time and time again: Claire would make something because she felt the desire for it, or the need of it herself—only to discover that she had answered the wants and necessities of other women too. The things she designed didn't always catch on quite so quickly as the Algerian dress had; sometimes, optimistically, she would show her new ideas and they would be ignored, or buyers would suggest that she modify her original ideas to something more ordinary. And sometimes she would withhold a garment, wear it herself— and find the orders piling in.

Almost always, once her ideas reached the consumer—the actual wearer of clothes—the women who worked and played as actively as Claire did herself recognized their charm and their advantages. But frequently they would be held up by buyers too timid to take a chance on things far outside the usual limits. More recently, of course, that is seldom true. Buyers have come to recognize the fact that Claire's designs aren't novel for the sake of novelty alone, acceptable only to the most adventuresome customer and therefore not practical for quantity purchase. There is always a reason for their strangeness, and it is usually a pretty sound reason.

When Claire was asked where her ideas come from, she answered simply, "From solving problems." And the designs for which she has become famous are, each of them, obvious examples of the truth of that statement.

Those boat trips to Paris, for instance, were likely to be cold and damp. So, regardless of the fact that French designers were making all their evening wraps of velvet and lamé then, Claire made one for herself out of tweed. She still wears it, and similar evening coats are worn today all over the country. They just make sense, that's all. They solve a problem.

Similarly, Claire became aware of the difficulties that sunburn presented. She hated the sight of those apparently inevitable white streaks that straps left across tanned shoulders. And she hated a lot of the other minor irritations that could turn a day at the beach into an exasperating experience. She decided to tackle them all at once. Starting out with a pale beige wool jersey (it looked nice against sand, and it was comfortable after a cold swim), she made a bathing suit with detachable straps that could be removed with a flick of the finger when one left the water. And then she made a coat dress of the same material to cover it. She could wear the dress to the beach, unbutton it and slip it off, and spread it out to lie on. And there was a huge pocket in the dress that carried the sun-tan oil and the make-up items that had always previously demanded a bag of their own, or gotten lost in the sand.

"Everything worked," as she put it. And of course it worked for sand-and-sea lovers everywhere as well as it did for her.

Then one day she discovered, somewhat to her own surprise, that she was really interested in cooking. She wanted to be in the kitchen herself when she was having guests, and yet not look too much like a cook when she came out to join them. So she made herself a kitchen dinner dress, with an apron to match. Very much to *their* surprise, the smartest magazines found themselves showing pictures of aprons in their austere pages. Aprons were sensible—women hadn't needed Claire to point that out. But they were grateful for her sensible suggestion that they could be smart and pretty too.

Once at a ski resort she saw a woman wearing an ice-blue satin evening gown, and it seemed terribly wrong to her even if ice-blue satin was popular that year. A ski resort wasn't a steam-heated city hotel. It was an oasis in the midst of acres of snow, and even if the fireplaces were blazing, there were draughts in the halls. Who wanted to see an animated icicle in that setting? The sight of it chilled the blood all over again, just as it was beginning to thaw out. And, for that matter, the poor wearer must be suffering herself, in that thin material and with her arms bare.

Claire went right home and sat down with her drawing pencil. The dress that emerged was of soft wool, long sleeved and snugly cosy. While she was at it she did another one in white wool, because it had occurred to her that ski lodges weren't the only chilly places in winter; stone churches could be pretty cold too, and a red nose and shaking blue hands were not becoming to brides.

A couple of years later, when houses and schools were likewise cold, from war-time fuel shortages, Claire put bright knee-length wool shorts, matching wool blouses, under wrap-around skirts; and college girls relaxing in their rooms could be ready for classes or the street in the twinkling of an eye—and warm wherever they were. She also fostered the leotard —that long-sleeved, long-legged and footed garment that dancers wear, and that so much resembles a child's footed pajamas. But it didn't look like a child's pajamas or a drab pair of tights when Claire was finished making it up in vivid figured jersey, to be worn alone or under a sleeveless jumper.

Just as logically, when summer came, she made some of the first of the very frankly bare-back dresses. To be warm in winter and cool in summer—wasn't that what women wanted? Then why shouldn't they have clothes that achieved that end?

Examples like this could be cited indefinitely, but it's about time to mention that best-known of all McCardell designs— the one which all by itself would have made her famous. *Harper's Bazaar* started her off. It was the year when maids were leaving domestic jobs for factories, and a lot of women were consequently doing their own housework for the first time. Their principal concern previously had been to look smart and attractive, and they still wanted to look that way, even if they now had to do the dishes and the dusting. So the magazine editors asked Claire to design something for them to wear.

Characteristically, Claire obliged with a dress that all women, rich and poor, accustomed to housework or not, took to their hearts. She made what came to be called the "Pop-over." It worked like a smock, fastening simply in front; it was easy to slip into and could be worn over an afternoon dress for last-minute jobs in the kitchen or by itself, for a full day's work, and it was of sturdy denim that laundered easily and flattened out on the ironing board when it had to be pressed. It solved a lot of problems, all at once. It worked, and women worked *in* it by the thousands.

In fact, they liked the casual, wrap-around style of it so well that Claire did dresses in that same design in wool and other fabrics for more formal wear. She had given birth to a real American classic.

Her use of denim in the Pop-over was only one expression of her approval of that material. "I'd always wondered why women's clothes had to be delicate—why they couldn't be practical and sturdy as well as feminine," Claire said. So she proved that they could be, in a variety of ways. She made tailored denim suits, that looked as well in the city as in the country, and denim shorts and slacks, and even long denim dinner skirts to be worn with gay cotton blouses. She used butcher linen too, because it also had the qualities she wanted.

The comfort and ease of men's clothes attracted her, and she borrowed a lot of ideas from them. Not the stiff tailoring—Claire has never cared for that—but the big pockets on jackets, the hip pockets, the soft trouser pleats, shirt sleeve shoulders, and the wearable, easily-laundered shirt material itself. From that sturdiest of all men's wear—work clothes—she borrowed blue jean stitching, and made it so glamorous that Fifth Avenue and the farm united in their acceptance of it.

Solving a problem also resulted in her six-piece interchangeable wardrobe, of skirt and jacket, blouse and slacks, and shorts and halter or gay brassière top. In denim, in black or white butcher cloth, in any of a variety of materials and designs, they offered infinite changes of costume for little traveling space. They comprised a complete wardrobe for a weekend in the country, or for a brief luggage-restricted plane trip. They worked.

Claire picked up a long, hooded wool peasant's cape in France, and brought it home to wear herself—and started another fashion. She saw women who had traveled in the Austrian Tyrol bring home the gay peasant dirndls, and wear them at their country homes, and she saw the dirndl copied widely in this country. Girls loved them—so well, in fact, that they frequently appeared in their cotton dresses when a more formal attire would have been usual. So Claire gave them dirndls in other materials, in silks and wools and rayons, as comfortable as they wanted and as much fun to wear, but adaptable to all occasions.

The dancer, Zorina, wanted an exercise suit, so Claire did her one in red jersey, with a whirling skirt. And before Zorina could do a dozen pirouettes, the ballerina bathing suit fad was underway.

War-time cloth shortages made it imperative for women to make-over and make-do, so Claire made patches smart instead of shameful by showing how to use them deliberately and colorfully.

Claire McCardell is no longer a designer whose name is

known only in the trade. People who wear her clothes have found out about her, and they seem to feel as if they know her—as indeed they do. They know that she understands the sort of clothes they need, and they have learned to look to her when new living conditions make other sorts of clothes necessary. Stores recognize that friendly feeling she has aroused, and are quick to advertise her designs not merely as something new, but as Claire McCardell's "something new." They do it with a reflection of the warmth that this young designer seems to arouse.

"Wouldn't you know she'd do it?" one store ad demanded of its readers. "Who? Claire McCardell, of course. Do what? Take a common garden variety of cotton, give it an avocado pear sophistication, turn it into the slickest little 'dude' suit that ever strolled out to meet a city summer."

That's how they write about her, because Claire's personality gets into her clothes. And, since it is so very much that typical American personality *Vogue* early credited her with, her clothes are beloved by American women. They're inexpensive, too. Those girls-with-little-salaries are never very far from her mind, and she salutes their good taste and pampers their pocketbook every time she sits down to tackle a new problem.

Consequently there were many people who approved the choice of Claire McCardell, in 1944, as recipient of the second annual Coty prize awarded by the American Fashion Critics to the designer most influential in her effect on fashion trends during the past twelve months. Americans approve of what she has done to fashion trends, and they hope she'll go on influencing them.

Her success is her own triumph, but a lot of people wearing McCardell clothes at their work or their play, insist upon congratulating themselves on it too.

SIX

NORMAN NORELL

There is a legend in the Norell family that runs as follows: one day, when Norman Norell was about three years old, his mother was strolling with him through the quiet tree-lined streets of Noblesville, Indiana, where the family lived, when suddenly Norman rose up in his carriage with a dreadful howling. Mrs. Norell, looking anxiously about to see what had disturbed her son, discovered the child's wide eyes fixed on a hat in the window of a little shop they were passing. It was a large hat, even for those days of enormous millinery, and it was trimmed with huge bunches of red cherries. A three-year-old might well have been frightened at the sight of it. But when his mother was finally able to interpret those vociferous yells, she realized that Norman wasn't frightened at all. He was screaming because he wanted her to *buy* that hat. He liked it. And so, the story goes, Mrs. Norell did.

Norman Norell doesn't remember the incident and he rather suspects his parents—as we all do under similar circumstances—of embellishing a family joke through the years. But this slender dark-haired man, frequently characterized as the "dramatist of New York's designers," admits that the story doesn't sound too unlikely. In other words, he says,

NORMAN NORELL

AN APPRENTICESHIP AT STAGE=
COSTUME DESIGNING SHAPED NORMAN NORELL'S EARLY
TENDENCY TOWARD THE DRAMATIC. NOW HIS CLOTHES
DRAMATIZE THEIR WEARERS BY MEANS OF STRIKING SIM=
PLICITY.

HOYNINGEN-HUENE PHOTO, COURTESY HARPER'S BAZAAR

NOT EVERY WOMAN CAN
WEAR NORMAN NORELL'S UNCOMPROMISINGLY DIRECT
CLOTHES, BUT THOSE WHO CAN ARE, LIKE NORELL FASH-
IONS, UNFAILINGLY REMEMBERED.

he did acquire early in life a lot of frequently strange ideas about what people should wear; and, owing to the fact that he was ill so much of the time when he was a child, his whims were catered to perhaps more than was good for him.

"Mother always claimed she was never able to wear that hat—that she'd bought it just to please me," he says. But she did, he adds, wear pretty extreme things just the same. And he believes his own first curiosity about clothes was aroused by her unusually lively interest in such things.

"You know," he explains, "there is one woman in almost every little town who is something of a freak as to what she wears. My mother was Noblesville's. She wasn't afraid of styles that looked new and rather daring, and she was more pleased than embarrassed when people talked about her clothes. She subscribed to all the fashion magazines, including the French ones, and one of my earliest recollections is seeing them lying around all over the house. So, though Noblesville had a population of only about five thousand people, and you might not think it would be a good place to learn about fashion, I had my mother and the magazines to teach me, and that was a good deal."

His numerous childhood illnesses gave him plenty of time to absorb such an education. He was out of school as often as he was in, and there were long stretches when he could do nothing more strenuous than lie in bed looking at pictures. Even when he was well enough to be out of doors, he could seldom take part in really vigorous games, and his older brother wasn't exactly enthusiastic over taking the baby along when he himself went out to play. So Norman's outings often consisted of sedate walks with his mother when she went shopping, or visited her dressmaker.

He doesn't seem to have felt sorry for himself, though. "I thought it was interesting to find out how clothes were put together," he says.

When Norman was five years old—he had been born in 1900—the family moved into near-by Indianapolis, where Mr. Norell's men's hat shop was located.

"Indianapolis was a wonderful place in those days," he remembers. "I don't know exactly why, but it seemed to attract more than its share of cosmopolitan things. At a time when many other mid-western cities were rather ordinary and dull, Indianapolis had several smart restaurants, lots of good shops, and several theaters. My mother didn't seem so much of a freak any more—there were a good many women in Indianapolis who dressed fashionably. The shops imported beautiful fabrics and trimmings—I can recall some of them even now—and a few of them even brought over French hats. I don't actually think those hats sold very well; they were pretty extreme even for that town. But they'd be imported for their prestige value, put on display for a while, and then eventually marked down to very reduced prices. And mother would buy them up.

"It was a grand city for the theater, too. All the road companies stopped there on their tours, we had pre-New York openings sometimes, and there was always the vaudeville—good vaudeville—on the Keith Circuit.

"My father took ads in the theater programs," he explains with a grin, "so we always had passes to everything. We'd see two, sometimes three or four shows a week. The family let me go, even when I was small—spoiling me again, you see—and our neighbors were always shocked that the Norells allowed a youngster to stay up until midnight just to go to the theater. But I loved it."

And he decided then and there, although nobody took him seriously, that when he grew up he was going to design costumes and sets for the stage.

When Norman was twelve he had to spend a whole long year in bed. As usual, he read vociferously, anything and everything. And the following year, when the family built a new home on the outskirts of town, he announced that he had worked out the decorations for his own room. Could he have it exactly the way he wanted it? Perhaps his parents wouldn't have agreed if they'd waited to learn what he had in mind, but as usual they'd already said yes.

He'd been reading a lot about the East, and oriental art, and his decorative scheme was a fabulous conglomeration of all the colorful new impressions in his mind. It might have looked well on a stage—it probably *was* on a stage, in Norman's imagination—but it was admittedly unusual for a respectable mid-western home.

Mr. Norell had had the walls covered in burlap, regarding that as a practical and, for those days, sufficiently novel decoration for a boy's room. But it didn't fit into Norman's plans, so he had the burlap painted over—in gold.

He laid a black carpet on the floor, had pieces of wood carved to represent pagodas and fastened them up over each window, and hung gold curtains beneath them. But his principal pride was his bed. It was round, about eight feet in diameter, and covered with a bright red cloth.

"My family was surprised at the whole thing," he recalls, "but they were really embarrassed about that bed. They were afraid people would think I was absolutely crazy. My father always told visitors that I'd wanted it that shape so I could never get out of it on the wrong side. He knew I'd never thought of such a thing—as a matter of fact I don't know why I wanted a round bed; I just did—but he was trying to make me sound at least a little more sensible than I was. It was awful, the whole thing." And then he smiles. "But I thought it was great."

That probably wasn't the only time the indulgent Norell family was embarrassed by Norman's fanciful ideas.

"I really was crazy on the subject of shoes," he says. "For a while I spent practically my whole allowance on them. I remember a black patent leather pair, with pearl grey uppers and pearl buttons; and one made of some black and white checked material, lined with red satin. Where'd I get them? I don't know. I found them somewhere in the stores. I told you, Indianapolis was wonderful in those days."

And then there was the high school fraternity dance, made memorable by Norman's determination not to own or wear a dinner jacket. He just didn't like the things. So he found a girl who said she didn't like evening dresses, either, and together they planned their protest appearance. The girl wore a sport skirt, with a bright green blouse and a visored cap. And Norman had on a black suit and a vivid red shirt. They were, he admits, a sensation.

Summing up his youth with a half-amused, half-apologetic murmur, he says, "I got away with murder."

In the meantime he was doing not very outstanding work in high school, and markedly undistinguished work in his art classes. Still lifes, with blue pitchers and apples, were not his idea of fun. He insisted that he was interested in art, but not on such a—well, undramatic—scale.

Strangely enough, for one who had rebelled at the uniformity of dinner jackets, Norman was tremendously eager to get into a perfectly ordinary drab khaki uniform when America entered the First World War. He was too young to enlist, however, so he insisted upon the next best thing: a military school. His family had been hoping that he would finish high school creditably and go on to college, as his brother had already done; but Norman had upset their plans for him too often in the past for them to be much surprised at his decision now.

When the armistice was signed, however, his interest in warlike matters flagged abruptly, and he came back home.

FASHION IS OUR BUSINESS

Naturally enough, his family wanted to know what he intended to do with himself. They were clearly prepared for something outlandish, and apparently resigned to approving almost anything he suggested. Some day, they hoped, Norman would settle down; and if it was going to be necessary for him to get a lot of foolish ideas out of his system first, the sooner he tried them and found out how foolish they were, the better off he'd be.

Norman had already taken some classes at the Art Institute in Indianapolis. Now, he said, he wanted more of the same sort of thing, but in New York. So at the age of nineteen, and with his parents' blessing, he left to enroll in the Parsons School. And the next summer he came home again.

Nobody was much surprised, except Norman himself. This shilly-shallying was what others had come to expect of him. But Norman had had every intention of completing his course, until he found that "the school had a lot of set ideas that I didn't agree with."

"In the painting class, for example," he explains, "we had to color complexions with a certain mixture of paint—that mixture and nothing else. I couldn't see it. I thought there were lots of different kinds of complexions. And there were other things like that, that bothered me. So I left."

He found a partner and opened a batik shop, there in Indianapolis. The young shop owners tied-and-died their scarves and materials themselves, and they were fairly successful at it. But in the fall they closed up. And once more people shook their heads.

Norman then declared that he was going back to art school. But to a different school, he added, before anyone could regard his decision as evidence of a new stability. And that fall he enrolled for the regular fashion and art courses at Pratt Institute.

His letters home said he didn't like the art classes, and the Norells waited for him to turn up again, like a bad penny. But this time Norman stuck. He didn't enjoy drawing vases and apples any more than he had in high school, but he was finding other parts of the curriculum pretty satisfying.

He was, in fact, and for the first time, finding what he'd always been looking for. In his own mind he had never been, as he seemed to others, aimless and without ambition. It was simply that the things he was interested in were rather unusual for a boy of his age and background, and he hadn't known exactly how to go about expressing and educating those interests. Now he was learning how to do just that.

When the students at Pratt were invited to submit entries in a contest for a blouse design, Norman entered and won. It was his first prize, and although he recalls it as being $100, he speaks as if it had been a million. In any case, it meant a good deal more to him than any actual amount of dollars and cents. It was justification. Heretofore the sketches he scribbled had appeared, to others, at least, mere idle fancies to amuse himself with, until he was ready to settle down.

FASHION IS OUR BUSINESS

Now he had in his hands a real check—money that would pay for food and room rent. And now he could say to others as well as to himself that perhaps his crazy ideas were in themselves something he could settle down to.

Shortly afterward he entered another contest, this time for stage costumes. He didn't win, but someone connected with the Keith Circuit saw his designs and sent for him. That meeting didn't amount to anything either, and Norman might have felt discouraged as a result. But he had had the satisfaction of talking to somebody who knew a good deal about the stage, and who had believed that young Norman Norell was worth investigating. Even though he hadn't been offered a job, he felt that the incident proved he was on the right track.

Determinedly he finished his course, right up through the final examination. And, almost immediately thereafter, fortune seemed to reward him. He met two men who were working in the very field that he wanted so much to enter. They were Gilbert Clark, formerly associated with the dress house of Henri Bendel and at that time owner of his own establishment; and Herman K. Smith, who was connected with the young movie industry then beginning to flourish in Astoria, Long Island. They both liked Norman, and they believed in him. And almost before he knew it, he found himself working on the clothes for a Rudolph Valentino picture, "The Sainted Devil." Mrs. Valentino and Adrian were both employed on the same job, and for the first time Norman enjoyed the sensation of doing work he liked, among people whom he understood and whose interests coincided with his.

Now all his youthful evenings at the theater began to bear fruit. He had only to shut his eyes and transport himself back to one of those performances in Indianapolis, to know what sort of thing caught a spectator's eye and held it. And a Valentino picture was an excellent opportunity for putting into practice dramatic ideas.

When the picture was finished, Norman's luck held. The glamorous Gloria Swanson came out to Astoria to play in a motion picture version of the stage success, "Zaza," and Norman did her costumes. After that he did some designs for Mae Murray. Even Indianapolis, he felt, would have to admit that dressing these popular stars was a mark of practical as well as artistic achievement.

Next came an offer to do the costumes for Murray Anderson's "Greenwich Village Follies," and almost simultaneously he was asked to work on the current "Ziegfeld Follies."

Even in a period when the world belonged very much to youth, Norman Norell seemed a remarkably fortunate young man. He was living in Greenwich Village at the time, and it was then regarded—by its own residents, at least—as the center of all that was lively and progressive in the field of the arts. Most of the people he knew were, like himself, busily engaged in creative work. In the fresh air of freedom that characterized the post-war '20's, they stimulated and encouraged each other. Life, on the whole, was more than satisfactory; and the Norell star was clearly in the ascendant.

And then, suddenly, things began to go wrong. The audiences that attended both the Follies shows were appreciative enough, and their applause had seemed particularly heartening to a young man whose father had steered guests hastily away from the sight of his son's bedroom only a few years before. But, appreciative or not, they were scarcely numerous. The shows were losing money. Norell was to be paid for his work when the books showed a profit, and it appeared that there was to be no profit.

It was difficult to go on feeling quite so successful under the circumstances. Surely the shows wouldn't be failing unless something was wrong with them; and it must have seemed possible, to a sensitive young designer, that the fault could be his. In any case, there loomed the unpleasant possibility that no one else would offer a job to a man who had been associated with two unsuccessful productions. Even the surest talent, faced by figures in red ink on the wrong side of the ledger, feels less sure of itself.

And then, before Norman had a chance to pull himself together and make a new start, he took sick. Illnesses had always been serious with him, and this one was no exception. He had no strength to resist when his family, learning of his condition, came East to take him back home. Probably it was just as well. Even with his mother's best care, he didn't recover for more than six months.

Doubtless, in most people's eyes, Norman's whole New York adventure thereby assumed the meager stature of his previous whims. Like the season at the military school, and the batik shop that lasted for a single summer, it must have seemed another notion enthusiastically conceived and readily forgotten. But, once more, people who thought that misjudged him. He did know what he wanted, as he always had. And as soon as he was well enough, he returned to New York.

One of his first visits was to the famous old Brooks Costume Company. People there always knew what was going on in the theatrical world, and perhaps they could advise an eager young designer how to get back to his trade. Unfortunately they couldn't. All the shows then being prepared for Broadway had already signed up their designers.

Norman, about to leave, was stopped by a kindly voice. "But we've got an opening here," it said, "if you're interested." Kiviette, soon to become a well-known designer herself, had just resigned from her job, and they would need someone to take her place.

Norman considered. It wouldn't be so exciting as the work he had done earlier. It was, in a way, a step backward. People who worked for Brooks didn't get their names on theatrical programs. But they did get paid salaries; they had the chance to absorb enormous amounts of information from men and women who were masters at their business; and they could learn how to design costumes by designing hundreds of them instead of dozens. By this time Norman had discovered that success achieved overnight was not necessarily lasting. So he accepted the offer, and settled down to the long job of climbing to the top the hard way.

Charles LeMair did the designs for the important shows that Brooks costumed, and Norman was assigned the smaller, less important productions. For several years he put in long hours a day at his drawing board, achieving costumes that would never be seen by a single one of the theatrical critics whose comments could lift a designer to fame. He did dresses for show girls in cheap burlesque houses, costumes for the chorus of the Cotton Club when it was still a comparatively obscure place in Harlem, wardrobes for vaudeville teams which never got nearer to Broadway than Brooklyn.

But Norman had always liked vaudeville, and now he enjoyed his association with it. The shows he designed had to be inexpensive, but that was no reason, he felt, why they should be drab and colorless. It was fun to design costumes that would go out on the Keith Circuit, and perhaps set other youngsters—as earlier shows had set him—to dreaming of all that was beautiful and exciting in the world. There was as much pleasure in that as there was in designing things for the "Ziegfeld Follies," whose audience was already accustomed to all the beauty that a great city had to offer. Perhaps there was even more. And there was satisfaction, too, in having each week a brand new job to do. Norman worked hard and liked it. And he learned a lot.

One day Charles Armour, owner of a wholesale dress house, offered Norman a job designing with him. He had seen Norman's things and he thought the young designer had a certain flair that he could utilize.

In a way Norman hated to leave Brooks. But Armour offered him a larger salary than he had been receiving, and he likewise offered an opportunity to do a new kind of work—to design clothes for private life rather than for life behind the footlights. It seems likely that the second fact influenced him as much as the first.

He worked with Armour for three years and a half, and before the end of that time he had begun to win something of a name for himself in his new field. His reputation owed itself as much to his ignorance, he says, as to his years of training in the designing of costumes. He didn't know anything about ready-to-wear clothes, and consequently he didn't know how many things were considered impossible. So he just went ahead and did them. Consciously as well as unconsciously, he carried over into the clothes he sketched something of the glamour and drama that he had been putting into his designs for the stage. Women liked what his clothes did for them.

Finally Hattie Carnegie offered him a place on her staff, and Norell accepted. Now he could, if he chose, consider that he had reached pretty close to the top of the ladder.

FASHION IS OUR BUSINESS

Some of the best and most expensively dressed women in the world would appear in the clothes he designed. Norman Norell was associated with one of the biggest houses and one of the biggest names in the business. He did, as a matter of fact, remain there for thirteen years. At the end of that time, knowing only that he very much wanted a place of his own, he left.

He didn't have enough money to finance such a thing himself, but a good many people who knew and admired his work had indicated that they would be more than glad of an opportunity to invest in the Norell future. Unfortunately, however, now that Norell had created that opportunity, they all seemed to disappear.

The designer could have taken a job in another house, but he hung on awhile, waiting, knowing what he wanted and determined to find it if that was at all possible. And finally he met Mr. Traina, owner of A. Traina Gowns, a house known for its superb workmanship.

"Mr. Traina struck me right away as being different from all the other people I'd been talking to," Mr. Norell says. "He didn't promise me the world, as they had done—just before they faded out of my life altogether. He talked down-to-earth common sense. I liked what he said, and I liked him. I decided he was somebody I'd like to do business with."

Apparently Mr. Traina had no difficulty coming to the same decision about Mr. Norell, and so the firm of Traina-

Norell was founded, in 1941, with Mr. Traina handling the business end and Norman doing all the designing.

Now, for the first time, he was completely on his own. Those long years of training and of application to a variety of jobs had produced a definite personality, and almost immediately it began to make itself felt in the fashion world.

One of his first successes was a black and white checked silk dress. The idea behind it was incredibly simple, but women had been wearing fussy, pretty prints in summer for so long, that the tailored plainness of black and white was a refreshing novelty. Suddenly, all over the country, simple checked and plaid dresses appeared, and they became almost a uniform for hot-weather wear, as adaptable to city life as to country vacations.

Then there was the suit with polka-dot accessories. A dot is undoubtedly the simplest design in the world, and Norell likes it for that reason. But, once again, its very simplicity makes it more dramatic than the most luxuriously-flowered pattern that was ever devised. And simple tailored suits, with scarves, hats or gloves in a polka-dotted material, lent women the dramatic quality of a clean sharp-lined etching.

Norell also designed a straight-lined chemise dress in pastel wool jersey, trimmed only with a row of jewelled buttons down the front—and another American uniform was born. The lines of the dress were easy and comfortable; the material was warm for cold-weather wear and yet it had the brightness under dark fur coats that only silk had formerly had; and the tiny jewelled buttons were the only trimming needed to point up and emphasize the softness of texture and shade, so they were the only trimming Norell gave them. The buttons actually buttoned, too. Norell has a vast distaste for buttons that have no functional excuse for their being.

He saw women faced with the new conditions of wartime living, and he reacted characteristically by driving straight to the point. Trailing evening dresses had always seemed an essential of every well-dressed woman's wardrobe; but trailing evening dresses became a liability when busses and subways replaced private cars and taxis. So Norell designed a new kind of dinner dress; it was bright with sequins, in order that no woman need feel cheated of that special sense of luxury that she associates with important evenings; but it was street length, so that she didn't have to bunch it up ridiculously in her hand as she made her way along slushy streets. And he made slacks out of soft, pliable furs, for chilly evenings in unheated houses. Of course nobody had ever seen fur slacks before; but if wool slacks were feasible, and if fur was even warmer than wool—then why not fur slacks?

Norell's attitude toward designing, like his designs themselves, is rooted in reasoning as clear and direct as that. And in one short year it won him the admiration not only of American women, but of that august body, the American Fashion Critics, who awarded him their first annual Coty prize for the important trends he had introduced during the past twelve months. They had recognized the fact that Norell's "crazy ideas" weren't necessarily so crazy after all. His clothes were as dramatic as the black suit with the red shirt that Norman had worn once to a high school fraternity dance; but, like that suit, they were founded on a belief that clothes should be both comfortable and becoming; and they derived their dramatic quality from a simplicity so marked that it seemed more striking than any amount of elaboration.

He doesn't like "frou-frou"—ruffles or jabots or what he regards as the pointless white bows and furbelows known as "lingerie touches." He doesn't like intricate cut for the sake of intricacy, and he doesn't use it "unless it has a darn good reason," as he expresses it. He believes that clothes should conform to the lines of a woman's body, rather than conceal or contort those lines; and for that reason he is particularly fond of wool jersey. "It sits to the body," he says; "it doesn't fight it."

He seldom uses prints, except for checked or striped or dotted materials; and most of those he does use he designs himself, usually in small geometric patterns.

Doubtless he found the restrictions of L85—the government war-time order regulating the hem measurement of a skirt to 72″ and the trimming material in each dress to half a yard—less of a burden than many designers. Pencil-slim skirts fitted neatly into the Norell tradition, and lack of trimming has always been a distinguishing mark of his clothes.

He likes shirtwaist dresses and has designed them in infinite variety. He likes pockets and he thinks women like them—but he uses them frequently because of his own preference for them, rather than theirs. This, incidentally, expresses a characteristic Norell point of view: he believes that he ought to attempt to design only the kind of clothes that appeal to him. Those, he thinks, are the only kind he will be able to do well. In his opinion, designers who attempt to please all kinds of women make a mistake.

"It seems reasonable to me that you can't possibly please everybody," he says, "and that if you try to do that, you're likely to succeed only in losing whatever originality you possess yourself."

If he makes it sound easy—this business of designing only what he likes—he is being unfair to himself. Designing clothes, as Norman Norell practices it, is an immensely demanding trade. Except for those brief periods four times a year, when one season's collection has been finished and the next one not yet begun, he lives on a rigid schedule that permits of almost no social life or recreation.

After a long day at his workroom, he goes home in the evening to his bachelor apartment on a quiet street in Greenwich Village. He takes his dog for a walk, has dinner, plays ball with the dog for a while, and then settles down to work.

"Sometimes it's an hour or so before I can draw a line," he says grimly. "But if I sit there long enough I always manage to produce something. I work until two or three in the morning, making from about twenty-five to fifty sketches in that period. They're pretty rough sketches—you remember, I said I was never much good at drawing—but my workmen and I can interpret them."

When he gets up the next day, frequently after only a few hours of sleep, he goes over all those drawings he made the evening before, and selects a few—sometimes only two—which cold daylight assures him are worth working on. Those few he takes with him, to the Traina-Norell offices on Seventh Avenue. And there they are made up by skilled workmen, usually in muslin. He spends the day himself studying and revising the muslin models that have been cut and stitched up from previous designs, inspecting final versions fashioned in the material for which the coat or suit or dress was designed, and choosing or designing trimmings, materials and accessories.

There are five models in the shop, and each dress is made up with one particular girl in mind. Unlike the models in many showrooms, these are hired on a year-round basis, so that they will be present for all the fittings and remakings that precede a showing. They are therefore also available for that other process that is an integral part of Norell work: the designing of the hats and bags and gloves that are to be shown with each garment.

"It always surprises me," Mr. Norell says, "to see how little attention most women pay to the ensemble effect of their clothes. They may buy a dress that suits them well—and then spoil it completely by wearing the wrong shoes, or carrying the wrong bag. Every item a woman wears must be considered in its relation to every other item, and that's why we show our models as we do—complete to every accessory.

"In my opinion," he goes on, "there should be just one *important* thing in each ensemble. If the hat is what I call important—that is, striking, attention-catching—then the dress and bag and shoes should be subdued in order to give it prominence, and to avoid a cluttered impression. The eye must have something to fasten on, and all other parts of the costume should lead the eye to that one thing."

One of the reasons many well-dressed women like certain Norell clothes is that they form an excellent background for their own jewels, or for a hat that needs the simplicity of a plain frock. But woe to them, in his mind, if they deliberately ruin a dress that is in itself "important," by superimposing upon it "important" accessories.

Even Sundays are not free in this designer's busy schedule. Those days he spends largely at the museums or art collections—sources which he thinks most people use far too little. The Museum of Costume Art, the Metropolitan and Brooklyn Museums of Art, are standard stops on his itinerary when he is on the search for ideas. And he still looks at the fashion magazines—the old ones, that is—as assiduously as he did when he was a child. When he finds something that he thinks might one day prove suggestive, he copies it carefully and stores it away in a drawer to be referred to weeks or months later when he has settled down for a long evening's work.

"I don't think a person can be a designer unless he or she is prepared, literally, to devote a lifetime to it," he says seriously. "Designing isn't something—at least it isn't for me—that can be done during the few short hours of a working day. It's a job that I work at continually. Even when I'm not at a drawing board, I'm constantly turning over possibilities in my mind—though I'm at my drawing board a good deal of the time. I don't get inspirations. My designs are pretty laboriously arrived at." Just, he might have added, as his success has been.

In spite of the opinions of those who knew him when he was a boy, he is probably as little subject to whims as anyone in the world. His whole life has been, even when appearances seemed to contradict this fact, a steady application of imagination and ability to the problem of designing that most difficult of all clothes: the simple dress that dramatizes its wearer.

He has been consistent in one other way too. That early interest in Chinese art has persisted through the years, and now his chief hobby, together with the buying up of eighteenth-century furniture, is prowling around looking for additions to his collection of Chinese jades and porcelains. But some day, he says, when he has time, he's going to start a collection of hats; he'll begin with those French models his mother bought so cheaply in Indianapolis. And he'll put in that hat with the red cherries on it, too, if it's still in existence.

SEVEN

JO COPELAND

Perhaps some day psychologists will conduct a survey among those people whom the world automatically classifies as successful, in order to find out how many of them regard their success as completely satisfactory. "Is it the way you thought it would be?" the questionnaire might ask.

Probably in a good many cases the answer would be no. Perhaps the famous lawyer would admit that as a boy he always rather imagined himself as an actor, declaiming Hamlet to an admiring audience; and perhaps the famous actress would reply that she landed on the stage almost by accident, while she was waiting for somebody to buy one of her paintings. But I strongly suspect that Jo Copeland, the sleek, smart designer for Pattullo Modes, would say, "Why, yes, of course. It's exactly the way I knew it would be."

Jo Copeland never allowed herself to be sidetracked. She could scarcely even have been discouraged very often. She just dreamed everything very clearly, and then she made her dream come true.

The essence of the dream could be expressed in a single picture, I think: the picture of a charming woman, in a luxuriously beautiful gown, posed against the background of a New York theater lobby on an important opening night.

JO COPELAND

JO COPELAND IS HER OWN MODEL, FOR SUAVELY ELEGANT CREATIONS BELOVED BY HER SORT OF WOMAN—THE YOUNG URBAN MATRON "WHOSE SOCIAL ACTIVITIES JUSTIFY A CONCERN WITH STYLE."

JO COPELAND'S GIFT FO
RESTRAINED ELEGANCE IS WELL ILLUSTRATED BY THE SLEE
BUT SOFTLY BECOMING LINES OF THIS SILK AND WOO
COSTUME.

Studying that picture carefully, she realized—as you do—that it had three elements. There was the woman herself, poised and groomed and confident; the dress she was wearing; and the glamorous occasion for which it was worn. But analysis was not enough. Her next task was to devise a method for transforming fancy into fact.

"Well," perhaps Jo said to herself, "I'm not that woman now—but I can be. The theater opening I don't have to worry about; such things happen all the time; they'll be waiting for me when I'm ready. As for the dress—"

Yes, the dress. That could be the link. The rest of the picture was for her irrevocably in the future. Growing-up took time. But the dress she could create immediately, at least in a pencil-and-paper version. She could draw the dress. It would be a beginning.

Jo drew a great many dresses. And now, wearing one of them herself, poised and confident and beautifully groomed, and attracting almost as much attention as the star at an important theatrical first night, she is a dream fully and completely come true. Hers is a Cinderella story clear-cut and happily-ended. And perhaps it proves—all fairy tales have a moral—that if you see your goal clearly enough, you will learn how to reach it; or perhaps it suggests that if you learn to do something superbly well, a grateful world may grant you the very setting you had always imagined as the background of your achievement.

But in either case—did you notice?—the word "learn"

seems an indispensable part of the conclusion. Cinderella had a fairy godmother to turn her pumpkin into a coach, but those convenient creatures are seldom available in real life. Certainly Jo didn't have one. She had to work her own miracle. And she had only her head and her fingers and her determination to aid her, but she would see to it that they were enough.

Jo was born and brought up in New York. Perhaps that seems a particularly fortunate beginning, but she scarcely recognized it as such at the time. She loved the city—she always has—but her family's ordinary, somewhat over-crowded house (there were nine children and Jo was the middle one) probably seemed to her as far from the world of her imagination as any small country town could have been. And her father was in the clothing business, but even that seemed no particular advantage. He was a jobber of women's suits and inexpensive clothes, and although she may unconsciously have absorbed knowledge of materials and manufacturing processes over the dinner table, she was in-clined to regard his occupation with some disdain. Those clothes had neither beauty nor elegance, and those were, as they are today, Jo's criteria.

But when her mother's seamstress "came in" at intervals to make the girls' clothes, Jo took a lively interest in what went on around the house. She fussed interminably over the dresses intended for herself. The fit must be exactly right. There must be no pointless, inappropriate trimming. If the neckline the pattern called for wasn't becoming, then the neckline must be changed, no matter how much trouble that caused. And, as Miss Copeland recalls now, it frequently caused a great deal indeed for both her mother and the dressmaker. But she says that she was probably even more of a nuisance when she designed a dress herself, and insisted upon its conforming exactly to her sketch.

Even so, with all her care, no finished dress was ever the sort of thing Jo was drawing constantly on all available scraps of paper and the margins of her books. It couldn't be, of course; she knew that. The things she drew were, from the very beginning, grown-up and luxurious. They were the sort of clothes worn to lunch at the Ritz, or to those evenings at the theater of which Jo dreamed.

Of course she often had difficulty reproducing exactly what her imagination conceived, so by the time she had finished grammar school she knew she would need to learn a great deal about art. Consequently she took special courses in it, at Washington Irving High School. She worked hard at them, and at her other studies too, and after graduation she took more art courses at the New York School of Fine and Applied Arts.

As a result she had no trouble finding a job, when she decided she was ready for one. She was hired as a commercial artist, and she was a good one. Now she could make the kind of drawings people wanted—ladies with pretty faces and anatomically correct figures. And, when she copied dresses, she could give them that indefinable something we call smartness.

Jo could have kept that job for a long time, but she had other ideas. She had never thought of it as anything but a necessary step toward her goal. Her father was pleased that she was working, because he believed that girls should be able to support themselves and be useful. But her salary wasn't vital to the family income, so he told her to keep it all for herself.

Jo saved almost every penny of it. She also took more courses, at the Art Students League in the evenings. And at the end of six months she announced that she was ready to go into business for herself.

She was still in her 'teens, and she didn't know anything about business. But Jo didn't care if people thought she was getting into something over her head. She knew just what she wanted to do and she was sure she could do it. She rented an office, big enough to set up her drawing board in, and found an agent who would handle her work on commission. It was up to him to discover people who wanted fashion drawings done, and to persuade them to let Jo try a few.

As she had expected, it wasn't too hard. She was a competent, careful artist. Customers who used her once were likely to use her again. By the end of the first month she was paying expenses, and had plenty of work to keep her busy.

But this too was just a step, and she was already looking ahead to the next one. So she found time, in odd moments, to make a few drawings in addition to the ones that had been ordered. These "extra" ladies wore dresses Jo had never been asked to copy. They were dresses that she had designed herself.

When she had a little collection of them done, she asked her agent to put them in his portfolio, and show them to the wholesale dress manufacturers he met on his rounds. Perhaps, she suggested, he might even sell one or two. If he thought his youthful client was over-optimistic, he soon learned otherwise. The drawings *were* salable. One manufacturer, the head of Pattullo Modes, was always willing to look at Jo's sketches and more and more frequently bought one for his own use. Finally he sent word that he would like to have Jo call on him.

He suggested, when she came, that it might be a good thing for her to give up commercial illustrating, and come to work for him. He would be taking a big chance, he pointed out; Jo was still a young girl. But she replied calmly that she would be taking a chance too; she was already earning over a hundred dollars a week at her one-woman business, and Pattullo hadn't, of course, offered anything like that amount as a beginner's salary. Finally they reached a compromise: Jo would work half the week for Pattullo, and half for herself.

It was an arrangement that protected them both. If she wasn't as good as he hoped (and as good as she herself believed she was), then neither of them had burned his bridges irrevocably. But she was good, of course. A short trial of the part-time schedule proved to Pattullo that Jo was a designer to keep, and proved to Jo that she needn't be afraid to close up her business. She had arrived.

To be a full-fledged designer at twenty was a remarkable achievement. To maintain the position she had won for herself was perhaps even more remarkable. Many promising youngsters don't fulfill the promise their early talent holds forth. Jo Copeland did because, from her youthful middy-blouse days, she had had a style and a philosophy of clothes. It had been the foundation of that dream. And now that the dream had become a reality, it was clear that it had always been based on something solid and real in Jo herself. All she had needed was the opportunity to express it—and Pattullo had given her that.

She had to go on learning, of course. One of the things she had to learn was that the elegance which had always been her goal did not depend upon elaboration. As a youngster she had been, perhaps, rather inclined to overdo things. She had enough confidence in herself to cut directly into expensive materials. (She never works in muslin first, because so much of the effect she wants depends on texture and drape.) But now she acquired sufficient additional confidence to rely on simplicity. And the simpler her dresses became, the more convinced she was that she was on the right track.

As the Pattullo designer, she made the regular designer's trips to Paris, and she visited the fashionable resorts and all the fashionable places in New York she had once imagined so vividly. Her good memory was a constant asset. She could always recall the detail that set one dress apart from a dozen others, or the particular line or color or treatment that had impressed her. She collected buttons, trimmings, materials and laces. And, even more avidly, she collected information, digested it, catalogued it, and had it at her finger tips when she needed it, ready to be freshly expressed in her own terminology of elegance.

She was disappointed in her first sight of Paris clothes. But though she educated herself to an appreciation of their perfection of cut, she felt that there was a basic fault in that perfection. French clothes were "complete without the woman." And always, as a child, when she had envisioned clothes, they were being *worn*. They were part of a picture of feminine beauty. That woman in her dream had had a face and a personality, and her dress suited her. So Jo set herself to design clothes on that principle.

As a result, her things were originally regarded in the trade as being difficult to sell. They "didn't look like anything in the hand." Even the wholesale buyers, supposedly trained to judge clothes, did not always appreciate Copeland designs. She recalls one well-known purchaser of dresses for a prominent midwest store, who visited the Pattullo showings for several days, and always left without placing an order. The staff grew curious. If she didn't like the clothes, why did she keep coming back? And if she did like them, why didn't she buy? Finally the mystery was solved. The buyer sat down beside Miss Copeland one day and asked her to explain which were likely to be the "good numbers" for her particular clientele. She had heard a lot about Jo's clothes, she said; she knew they were becoming increasingly popular among fashionable women. But she admitted that, for herself, she couldn't make any choice from a collection of dresses so confusingly simple—beautiful on the models, but a mere length of fabric otherwise.

So Miss Copeland explained, as she has frequently done before and since, her theory on the subject. Now such explanations are seldom necessary. But the change that fact implies is something she likes to talk about.

When the transition was originally taking place, she points out, from dressmaker-made clothes to ready-to-wear, women who demanded careful fitting and an unhurried study of each garment they bought had to search out the "little shops" where that kind of service was alone available. But gradually more and more women took a serious interest in clothes. They studied styles and they studied themselves, and they learned enough to be unsatisfied with a dress that expressed the fashion trends of the moment if it did not also suit their own personalities. They wanted to try things on at leisure, to see dresses in relation to their own figures and their own faces. So large department stores, always sensitive to their customers' wants, inaugurated their own "little shops," where a dress that "doesn't look like anything in the hand" could be given the attention it deserved.

But today this appreciation of clothes-as-an-adjunct-to-personality has become so widespread that even women who purchase from bargain racks study a dress before they buy it. They ask more than serviceability and a color that won't fade; they ask more than a lace collar and a splashy bow. And it is a tribute to them, Miss Copeland declares, that the majority of garments they have to choose from are designed with the foreknowledge that they will be given this close attention.

Now buyers and the public alike have learned the lesson Jo taught herself: that ornateness is not fashion, and that simplicity is its own elegance. Now a woman buys a dress because it is "her sort," because it conforms to her idea of herself.

And, naturally enough, Miss Copeland designs according to that principle. She designs for herself and the sort of person she is—chic, beautiful and fashionable, like the woman in the dream. Her clothes are expensive, and utilize expensive materials, but it is her contention that women who can afford such things are glad to pay the price.

"After all," she says, "a woman doesn't spend her money for cloth and a row of buttons. Cloth and buttons aren't worth the price she pays. But the look in her husband's eyes when he sees her in a new dress for the first time, and tells her she has never looked lovelier—that's worth a great deal. And she's willing to pay for it."

If that statement indicates that Copeland designs are intended for a single, dramatic appearance, it gives a wrong impression. She believes as firmly in adaptability as she does in simplicity. A dress must make a woman look lovely for as long as it lasts. It ought not to be so extreme in cut that its usefulness fades with the waning of a single fashion season. And it must be wearable for a variety of occasions—wearable in the sense of comfortable and becoming and suitable.

Miss Copeland is perhaps as well known for her suits as for any other one thing. She introduced the fashion of the dressmaker suit, complete in itself, without a blouse. But when her suits do have blouses, she demands that the outfit "have the significance of a dress" when the jacket is removed. She likes silk suits—of printed crepe, for example—as well as she likes wool ones, and believes they are equally useful. She prefers soft lines to severe tailoring, and insists that even suits have a softness at the throat. "But no frills," she adds. Women, she thinks, should "look attractive but not sissy."

She works frequently with print designers, and is always searching for new and different print patterns. She finds them, too, or helps to create them herself. When most designers were depending chiefly upon Paris for their patterned material, Jo Copeland took American material to France, and had the pleasure of seeing them used by prominent designers there at a time when this country was considered incapable of producing such things.

She was also a pioneer in the custom of putting appropriate jewelry—clips, pins or necklaces—on the dresses she designed. It was an addition the customers appreciated, since they might not be able to find the suitable accessories for themselves. And it gave the designer more scope; she was not required to limit her fashion to frocks adaptable to a wide variety of ornaments.

A young matron herself—with two children of whom she is very proud—and urban to her fingertips, Jo Copeland designs chiefly for the young city matron "whose social activities justify a concern with style." And she herself enjoys city pleasures. She likes the theater—yes, first nights, of course—fashionable restaurants, entertaining and "watching people." She is always aware of clothes, and always consciously continuing her education in them, and in everything else.

She believes that "it is impossible for a designer to know too much about anything." She must be awake to all the new influences around her, and to the state of the world. History, economics, art—everything is and must be grist to her mill; they are not merely the source of occasional ideas; they are the foundation of all her ideas.

In spite of her sketching ability, Miss Copeland designs directly on the figure, and the figure she always uses is herself. You can see her any day, standing intently before the mirror in the busy Pattullo workroom (where she has remained since her first employment there, except for a few years when she operated a wholesale house of her own), pinning and draping and fussing until she gets just what she wants. She will be doing with a piece of material what she has done all her life: conjuring up a clear and specific dream, and then making that dream come true.

EIGHT

PHILIP MANGONE

As you will have gathered, if you read the earlier chapters in this book, one of the questions I inevitably put to the designers I interviewed went something like this: How did you choose your career—or did it just happen? But I knew better than to ask such a question of Philip Mangone, the famous designer and maker of women's suits, ensembles and coats. It was apparent within a few moments after I had met him that it could never have occurred to him to do anything other than he does.

His father, Francesco Mangone, was a tailor before him, and so were six generations of Mangones before that. Philip himself would be a baffling subject for any group of scientists trying to solve the age-old problem of the relative importance of heredity and environment; because both influences, as far as he was concerned, led him in the same direction. You might almost say he was born a tailor; and you could certainly say he grew up as one.

Francesco Mangone spent the early part of his life in southern Italy. According to the custom of the times and that country, he plied his trade by traveling from one wealthy home to another, staying long enough in each completely to outfit the womenfolk of the house. "I can remember my father telling me how he worked," Philip Mangone says. "He used to take his tailors, fitters and seamstresses with him, and they were all boarded and housed at the home where they were employed—noble houses, many of them. Usually each job lasted quite a while, because he made everything from corsets to dresses."

But finally, like so many of his countrymen, Francesco came to the United States. Here his great sense of style earned for him, from the first, excellent jobs as head tailor in various good establishments. Even so, things weren't always easy, because the family was large. Philip was one of six children, and the Mangones lived in rather crowded quarters in the section of New York known as Greenwich Village. It was a neighborhood heavily populated by Italians, and so, although Philip had been born in this country, he grew up among his own people and learned their merriment and their capacity for pleasure and enjoyment. Even the fact that he had to leave school when he had finished the eighth grade, didn't break the high spirit so characteristic of him today, more than half a century later.

He had had a taste of labor even earlier than that, actually, working after school each day on the great bundles of half-finished garments which clothing manufacturers of that period sent out to be done by workers in their own homes. At first he was trusted with only the simplest seams; but soon he was making buttonholes, and performing such tasks as putting on the numerous rows of stitching which formed

PHILIPPE HALSMAN

PHILIP MANGONE

PHILIP MANGONE HAS BROUGHT
TO A HIGH DEGREE OF PERFECTION THE FINE WORKMAN-
SHIP AND SENSE OF STYLE BEQUEATHED TO HIM BY SEVEN
GENERATIONS OF MANGONE TAILORS.

PHILIP MANGONE HANDLES
TWEED WITH AN UNFALTERING TOUCH, TO PRODUCE A
CHARACTERISTIC SUIT=AND=TOPPER COMBINATION.

both stiffening and trimming around the bottom of the popular flared bicycle skirts of the day. His first full-time job, however, was in the alteration rooms of the big Altman store, where his father was then employed.

Not long afterward father and son both moved to a wholesale dress house, and then to a similar, larger house owned by the then-famous Julius Stein. Still later they were both employed by the Harry Rothenberg and Levy establishment, and there Philip did his first designing.

He was still in his teens, but his association with his father had given him a very thorough training in all the aspects of his work. He already knew a good deal about wool, for example—one of the most important and most basic of all the tools of his trade. Francesco Mangone had been a good wool man—that is, he had been able to judge materials quickly and accurately, with a sharp eye and sensitive fingers. Philip learned to do that too. And he learned which materials draped most effectively, which could best be handled in one way and which in another.

When he was nineteen he made his first trip abroad, entrusted by his employer with the responsible task of choosing woolens from the European markets.

And of course by that time he also knew every detail of the precise and demanding business of tailoring. His hands were trained to cut and fit; he had been taught the importance of detail—the exact method for handling a piece of stiffening in a collar, for example—and of exquisite workmanship; and his mind and his eye had learned style and the trick of adapting the latest dictates of Paris to the American figure and to a certain standard of quiet good taste which was always to mark his own creations. Before he was twenty he was a tailor in every bone of his body. He could do everything that was needed to be done to create and complete a woman's suit or coat, from envisioning the finished garment in his mind's eye before the cloth had ever been cut, to fashioning the buttonholes and pressing the final seam.

The last house with which the two Mangones were both associated was that of Charles M. Cohen. There Philip did a great deal more designing. And finally, in 1916, he took over the business and set up for himself on Madison Avenue.

That was the period when the "ensemble"—a matching coat and dress, or a coat and dress specifically designed to complement each other—was being widely introduced in this country, and Philip found it an excellent form of expression for his talents. His knowledge of fabrics was such that he could combine them with unerring success; and the simplicity of line which had always been his own preference was particularly effective in such clothes. Furthermore, from the very beginning, he maintained such high standards of workmanship that women who demanded the best sought him out and willingly paid his always-high prices.

Since that time Mangone has continued to present a fine adaptation—fine in spirit and execution—of the newest style trends. He seldom originates, although he is credited with introducing the swagger coat and, later, the topper. In fact, his combination of suit and topper is a typical Mangone solution to the American woman's clothes problem. He believes, first of all, that a woman never looks better than she does in a well-made, well-fitting suit. In it she can be comfortable, groomed with the minimum of fussing, and appropriately dressed for almost any hour of the day. Suits can go anywhere, in Mr. Mangone's opinion—and his do. Combined with a topper, they form a wardrobe complete in itself and an almost infallible answer to the question of "What shall I wear?"

The suburban woman, coming into the city on a five o'clock train to meet her husband at his office and go on with him to dinner and perhaps to the theater—what better costume could she wear than a suit? And the businesswoman, wanting to be efficiently neat in her office and yet sufficiently well-dressed for restaurant dining—what better costume could *she* choose than a suit?

Mr. Mangone has such women in mind when he works. He gives them clothes that don't muss and wrinkle, that are simple enough for the most businesslike office or the most crowded train, and yet becoming and so beautifully made that they can appear proudly in any but the most formal setting.

Perhaps best-known for his classic, almost severe one-, two- or three-button suit, he also does a wide variety of softer, dressmaker suits. He feels that both types have their place in most wardrobes. His classic suits are "good" for years, because in them he reduces a season's innovations to the merest suggestion of a new shoulder line or jacket length. His softer suits, on the other hand, although never extreme, show more definitely the influence of style trends and satisfy feminine desire for last-minute fashions. They have, too, such flattering and dramatic touches as jet embroidery on collar or pockets, and beautiful and striking combinations of colors.

It was to Mr. Mangone that the authorities appealed when a uniform suit and coat was needed for the Women's Auxiliary Corps. When he had completed that designing chore, he turned out a series of coats in tweed, melton cloth and woolen coatings, all made on military lines. And the military coat, both long and short, was one of the most popular fashions of the period.

He likes capes, too, and most of his collections include at least one example.

Materials—woolens, usually—are his principal inspiration. He ranges over the wide sweep of the world's woolen markets, and often designs weaves himself, to be made up by some favorite manufacturer. Color and texture are equally important to him, and one or the other, or both, suggest to him the suit or coat which might be most effectively made from any given piece. It was his own idea, one year, to have rows of white "dashes" embroidered on navy or black wool; and he created a tremendously successful line of suits and coats from the finished fabric, inspired by the crisp contrast of its lines of broken white.

Ordinarily the majority of his ideas for fabric colors are derived, not from "the Persian," or "the Empire," or any other native or period style; but from nature. If, for example, a weaver sends him a beautiful piece of tomato-colored wool, he is most likely to combine with it a shade of green or a brown earth shade, to form a color symphony patterned after the basic color combinations in the world around him.

He likes fur both for its beauty and its utility, and uses it frequently. But the problem presented by skyrocketing fur prices in wartime was one he was eminently suited to solve. His knowledge of fabrics and his skill at handling them resulted in coats and suits wherein contrast was obtained, not with caracul or beaver, but with inserts or collars of another material, or the material of the garment itself so cut as to present an effectively different "face."

He works, usually, from sketches he does himself, or from sketches contrived by his assistants at his suggestion. The next step is a muslin model, and from it patterns are made for the actual manufacturing process.

The Mangone establishment is a huge one. Adjoining his present main office on Seventh Avenue is a large factory employing four hundred persons. Chief among them is smiling, white-haired Miss Minnie Neubauer—"Aunt Min" to everyone in the place—who joined the Mangone staff as a model when she was sixteen, and has remained ever since as Mr. Mangone's right hand.

On the same premises are the showrooms and workrooms of the Greco Blouse Company, a Mangone subsidiary where blouses of Mr. Mangone's design are made up for general sale and specifically to complement Mangone suits. His blouse designs prove that he is as much at home handling soft silks as he is with the heaviest tweed.

There are four other workrooms, scattered throughout the vicinity, where Mangone clothes are made. Their number is necessitated by a demand from retail stores all over the country—many of which have special Mangone departments devoted solely to his designs.

And then, uptown in the midst of the fashionable shopping district, Mr. Mangone maintains a studio where he does most of his creative work. He believes firmly in the importance of atmosphere, and feels that he needs beautiful surroundings to spur him to his best efforts. Similarly, he feels that although he likes good food, he can truly enjoy it only in attractive places.

Before the war he went to Paris four times a year, and he was there, the last time, until thirty days before Paris fell. He enjoys the stimulation of those trips and, when 1 saw him, was looking forward eagerly to going again. More of a pioneer in his traveling than he is in his fashion designs, he returned to the United States from Europe in 1937 on the famous Graf Zeppelin—and was almost fatally burned when the great airship exploded into flames as it landed in this country.

Women's styles have changed a great deal since Philip Mangone first left school to go to work. In his earliest days he made bustles and leg o' mutton sleeves. But he himself prefers the styles of today, with jackets molded smoothly to the uncorseted human figure, and skirts that are conveniently and becomingly short. In his opinion women too like this sensible style—like it so well that they will never again allow the leaders of fashion drastically to change their silhouette. It seems likely, though, that should styles materially shift, Mr. Mangone would be able to devise an adaptation of them to conform to the conservative good taste which so many well-dressed women rely on him for.

A craftsman to his fingertips, Mr. Mangone is an acknowledged leader in his own special field. One of the stores which features his clothes once expressed very well the particular gifts which Philip Mangone brings to the designing and making of women's clothes. It pointed out in an advertisement that one could always expect from him the "refinement of a trend—the perfection of a fashion creed." Indeed, perfection is his own creed. And those seven generations of Mangone tailors may well be proud of the master tailor who has come after them.

NINE

EDITH HEAD

In 1938 Edith Head was made chief dress designer at the big Paramount Studios, and thus became the first woman to hold that position in any of the major motion picture companies. She had been born in Los Angeles, California, the center of the movie industry, and thus it might at first glance appear as if a fortunate geographical accident had given her a sort of running start toward her success. But the truth is that her childhood removed her so very far from the movies, and indeed even from any educational opportunities that might seem a natural prerequisite to her eventual career, that it was almost an accident that she ever got into them at all.

Edith was an only child, and while she was still very tiny she was taken to live at a small Mexican mining town, where her engineer father was employed. It was a rather grim, lonely, dusty place, and Edith had no one to play with, and very few toys. So she amused herself by dressing and redressing her dolls, and even the little burros that were, she says now, her first "stars"—and her most patient. She doesn't know whether the burros objected to the bows she tied around their necks or not; but she does know that she learned then to love those quiet stubborn little animals, and that she loves them still.

EDITH HEAD

TINY, DYNAMIC EDITH HEAD, FIRST WOMAN EVER TO BE MADE CHIEF DESIGNER FOR A MOTION PICTURE STUDIO, DRESSES ALL OF PARAMOUNT'S SCREEN STARS.

EDITH HEAD'S DELIGHTFUL
FROCK FOR MARY MARTIN IS BURDENED WITH NONE OF
THOSE TOO=EXTREME DETAILS WHICH CAN DATE A DRESS
EVEN BEFORE IT APPEARS ON THE SCREEN.

When Edith was eight the family moved back to the United States, but they continued to live in various mining camps in Nevada and Arizona. Edith had learned Spanish in Mexico, she had picked up a good deal about mining and mining localities, and she knew something about Indians because the Heads sometimes lived in the middle of Indian Reservations. But there were never any schools near the camps, and, when her lack of formal education became a real problem, she was hurriedly tutored in all the subjects she had missed. And finally she was taken to Los Angeles to enroll in the high school there—a shy, uncertain little girl, far more at home with miners than with children of her own age, and fearful about her recently-acquired arithmetic and history.

Sensibly, she decided to concentrate upon the linguistic skill her unusual childhood had taught her, by continuing her Spanish. And, when she was graduated, she entered the University of California and eventually took an M.A. at Stanford University, still specializing in languages. She had, rather incidentally, taken art courses too. But when she was ready to get a job she forgot all about those and settled down to teach Spanish at the Bishop School in La Jolla, California. Not long afterward she took another teaching position at the Hollywood School for Girls.

In spite of her small size, Edith has a dynamic, clear-cut personality. Her black eyes beneath smooth black hair are bright and alive. People listen to her when she talks. So teaching was easy for her, and teaching languages was easiest of all. In fact it used up so little of her great supply of energy that she was soon looking around for some additional outlet. She began to study art again. She attended classes in sculpture, in life drawing, and in landscape and portrait painting in oils, at the Otis Art Institute and later at the Chouinard Art School in Los Angeles. And she amused herself in between times by making dozens of fashion sketches.

Some of her students at the Hollywood School for Girls were the daughters of stars and executives in the movie industry, and gradually Edith's interest in the studios increased. After she had visited them several times, it occurred to her that she would enjoy working in such a busy, hectic place. She packed up a collection of her sketches and took them over to Howard Greer, then head fashion designer at Paramount. And Mr. Greer took one careful look at them and gave her a job on the spot.

Edith was no longer a youngster, of course, and she had already had two good jobs. She took more or less for granted that this one was to be pretty good too. But she found herself relegated to the rather lowly classification of a sketch artist, and assigned as her first task the designing of an enormous waistband to support the palanquin on the back of an elephant. For a moment she must have been heavily tempted to return to teaching, where she had already established herself. But she had made up her mind that she wanted to do costume designing, and—well, she had once dressed burros, hadn't she? She supposed she could dress an elephant too.

That was in the days when Cecil B. DeMille was embellishing his productions with monumental mob scenes employing thousands of extras. So after the elephant was properly fitted out, Edith spent quite a while, day after day, designing costumes for those innumerable extras—costumes that would be seen only for the briefest moment, and then at a tremendous distance from the camera. But it was good experience, and it helped to teach her the one great principle of designing for the movies: that all clothes must suit the story and be subordinated to it. The men and women whose clothes she was sketching were not meant to be conspicuous; their role was to form a background for action. And Edith's costumes must contribute to that fact, not detract from it by allowing a striking dress to seize the attention of the audience.

And of course it was good experience from another point of view, too. DeMille productions were frequently historical, and Edith learned to work with and to know the clothes of many periods. She also, incidentally, had the opportunity to prove herself especially useful to her employer, when there was a necessity—as there often was—to do research in books obtainable only in French or Spanish.

After a while Edith was promoted to the more individual, if scarcely more flattering, field of the horse operas. And she dressed cowboys and cowgirls until the sight of a pair of chaps would have driven a less patient person to the point of frenzy. She kept at it, though, and had her reward when Travis Banton succeeded Howard Greer as chief designer, and Edith was made Banton's assistant. And, when Banton left in 1938 to become a free lance designer, Edith Head was given his place.

She was ready for the responsibility that was now resting solely on her shoulders. By that time she had not only received a thorough grounding in the specialized techniques of designing for the movies, but she had learned in addition just how elaborate and wearing a routine her work demanded. She knew that when a picture was announced, it was not enough to study the period in which it was laid, and the stars who were to play in it. She had first to read the script carefully, in order to understand the spirit of the story and its various characters. Then she must confer with the producer, the director, the art director, the cameraman, the stars and—when technicolor had made its appearance—with the experts in that aspect of the work.

Today she frequently has as many as three hundred sketchers, drapers, cutters and finishers on hand to carry out her ideas, but it is always her job to oversee them all and to see that the ideas *are* carried out. So she must know all about the types of work each of those people is doing, and she must be able to serve as an executive and a trouble-shooter as well. She must be ready at any hour of the day—or night —to formulate a master-plan for a star's entire wardrobe, or to take a single emergency stitch in a dress that causes trouble at the very moment when the cameras are beginning to grind.

Not long ago her studio released a report of a typical day in Edith Head's busy life. I think it might be well to quote it here:

"Arriving at her office at 9 A.M., she was called immediately to the set where Dorothy Lamour was working. A sudden decision had been made to send Lamour, who was wearing an evening dress, out into the snow from a "Road to Utopia" interior. Edith had to scare up a fur cape for her. That done she returned to her office, put a few finishing touches on key sketches and turned them over to her two sketch artists for enlargement. Then she went into the workroom to watch patterns cut for Veronica Lake, remembering first to send somebody scouting for pink spangles for another number.

"Came a phone call from the set where Loretta Young was working. Loretta had half an hour between camera set-ups and wanted fittings. Over went Edith with her crew of fitters. That session was interrupted by a call from Producer Paul Jones. He was fuming over a parka intended for Hillary Brooks. Said it made her look like a polar bear. Would Edith please rush right over? She did and soothed him by suggesting a dye job on the parka. At least, then, she said, it could only make Hillary look like a brown bear.

"Back to the workroom for more checking and then she

went to the Paramount dance bungalow where she watched rehearsals of a dance between Marjorie Reynolds and Billy Daniels, so she could plan Marjorie's costume.

"The noon hour was devoted to a Betty Hutton fitting. They lunched on sandwiches dispatched between pin-sticking. Nor was the afternoon any more restful. First there was a press interview, followed by examination of a mountain of samples to choose material for forthcoming productions, followed by a conference with technicolor technicians. They must approve every color used on every garment for color films.

"At 4 o'clock Edith went to a projection room. She sees the daily rushes of every film in production. Six o'clock found her in a fitting room waiting for Dorothy Lamour. Most fittings during production have to be conducted after filming hours, and this one lasted until seven."

Of course things wouldn't be so difficult for a studio designer if a studio worked on only one picture at a time. But that is seldom if ever the case, especially when the studio is a large one. When I met Miss Head she was working simultaneously on "one picture with winter clothes, one with summer clothes, one war picture laid in England, one post-war picture, one musical laid in Mexico—not to mention one 1902 and one 1885 film."

And each picture has its own very special problems, in addition to the thousands of problems that are more or less standard to every one. If the story is historical, there is a tremendous amount of research to be done. And if it is contemporary, Miss Head must keep in mind the all-important fact that by the time its star appears on the screen at your neighborhood theater, perhaps a year or more after her wardrobe for the picture has been designed, she must look well-dressed to your eyes, and up-to-date.

"I have to guess ahead," Miss Head explains, "so as not to use those outstanding current styles which might make the picture look old-fashioned when it is shown. What I really need is a ouija board."

What she has instead, of course, and it is far more reliable, is that particular style-sense with which all motion picture designers must be endowed. It's not wholly a gift, not just something you're just born with. It comes from a trained understanding of what is most basic and, principally, of what is most becoming in *any* current fashion. And it depends upon the intelligent application of that understanding to the variety of personality types which stars represent, both in their persons and in their screen roles.

It is more important, for example, as Miss Head explains, to dress Veronica Lake to emphasize her particular kind of beauty, her "style," than it is to make her a fashion plate for the country as a whole to follow. And if admiration for a star is likely to inaugurate a fad for what she wore in her last picture, that is not a factor which Edith Head can allow herself to take into consideration ahead of time. On the contrary, she is careful to point out, motion picture designers should not deliberately attempt to influence the styles of women in general. That isn't their job. Their job is to dress individual actresses for the characters they portray. And although Miss Head is happy if something she has designed for a leading lady proves suitable and therefore popular among women everywhere, she is shocked and chagrined whenever some extreme costume, intended to bring out the spectacular aspects of some particular role, is mimicked by women to whom it is not only unbecoming, but vastly unsuitable.

Take, for example, that first famous sarong which Miss Head devised for Dorothy Lamour. "There isn't another woman in Hollywood who could look regal in it," according to Miss Head. "If every woman looked as Dorothy Lamour looks in a sarong, I would say positively that the actress had started something. But such speculation leads to the question of how many women can wear such a simple little thing. And the answer to that, inevitably, is 'None.' "

Of course she has, since, designed numerous dresses for Dorothy Lamour based on the draped principle of the sarong, and many of them have earned nation-wide popularity. That's all right, from Miss Head's point of view; if you can wear draped dresses, wear them. But if you think you can wear a sarong, just because Dorothy Lamour looks wonderful in hers, she suggests that you think it over a little longer.

Historical pictures start fashion fads as often, if not oftener, than contemporary stories. There was the movie version of "Zaza," for one, made in 1938. In it Claudette Colbert wore numerous delightful costumes inspired by the 1904 setting of the story, and Miss Head predicted that many of their features would catch the public fancy. In fact, when she went to Paris herself that year she was gratified to find that style center already showing clothes suggested by her own "Zaza" costumes. They weren't duplicates, naturally; they were subtle translations of the more universally becoming lines and foibles of the period into modern clothes. High collars, long full bishop sleeves, shoulder yokes, ornamentation or flounces at the knee line, plaid taffetas and colored woolens, forward-perched hats and capes—those were the things that Miss Head was pleased to see other designers copy, and women everywhere wear. In other words, imitation is as pleasant a form of flattery in the designing field as it is anywhere else, but Miss Head doesn't like to see women foolishly attempting to flatter their favorite stars— and, they hope, themselves—by buying clothes which are inappropriate to their own physical characteristics and their own lives.

The years in which she has been in the motion picture industry have witnessed a change which bears upon this point, and which she feels is important enough to comment upon.

"In the 'good old days,'" she once wrote, "when designing was a cross between camouflage and costumes for 'Superman,' we dressed stars like nothing human. In fact, the rule was, if you could buy the dress in a store and wear it—if you *could* buy it—it wasn't a good 'picture dress.' I can remember a sheath of cut crystal drops I designed for Clara Bow; she couldn't sit down in it and she was pretty unhappy about the whole thing because it made her look a little like a chandelier. I can also remember designing a dress for Pola Negri that had a four-yard train of ermine tails—catching on everything on the set. This was too simple, so we added ermine tail earrings. One of our super-costumes was a little everyday riding habit for Irene Rich. Everything was pretty regulation except that we decided gold riding boots and a gold derby would give us a 'touch.'

"However, in extenuation of a studio designer, it wasn't only clothes that were unreal," she added. "Bathtubs were all gold, sets were all completely unlivable, and I don't think our stories were any too real. So I honestly don't mind when people say to me, 'Remember the *fantastic* clothes you used to design?' After all, it was the fabulous era and the movies were very young."

Edith Head gives credit to the wartime clothing regulation, popularly known as L85, for much of the improvement and toning-down that has come into movie designing. Studios were required to follow it as closely as dress designers and manufacturers were—and consequently they began to dress their stars in clothes more closely resembling the clothes that other people wore.

"It banished super-luxury and brought us all down to

earth," Miss Head told a *New York Times* reporter once. "How well I remember the day when we would swirl fox skins around the hem of a secretary's dress, or put a white satin uniform on a trained nurse. Now we hold to stark realism."

Because she is a pretty realistic person herself, this is completely satisfactory to her, and she thinks that on the whole it is satisfactory to audiences too. Once she refused to let a star wear a cloth-of-gold evening gown in her role as a working girl, and the star objected—on the grounds that the audience would. "But in real life," Edith pointed out to her, "working girls, with only their weekly pay checks to keep them afloat, can't wedge silver fox capes and lamé gowns into their clothes budgets." The star still wasn't convinced; she believed that her fans wouldn't notice the discrepancy between her screen salary and her screen wardrobe; she insisted that all they wanted was for their favorite actress to look glamorous.

"You should visit more neighborhood picture theaters," Miss Head retorted firmly, "and listen to the cynical comments of business girls and housewives concerning the elaborate wardrobes displayed by some of their screen counterparts. I can give you glamour and style without furs and sequins."

And that's just what she manages to do. So, nowadays, when a star is playing a contemporary role, in a story of everyday life, women can try to copy their clothes with far less risk of dressing foolishly and inappropriately than was formerly the case—provided, of course, they pay as close attention to their own "style" as Miss Head does to that of her various stars.

And she suggests that if you do feel compelled to follow the stars when you shop or sew for yourself, that you take the trouble first to decide which star you most closely resemble, and that then—within the limits dictated by your own common sense—you "do, or don't do, what she does, or doesn't do."

"No two people," Miss Head once said in an interview on this subject to a fan magazine writer,* "can look alike in the same thing. But if you are, let's say, the Veronica Lake type, you don't have to go completely off the beam by turning yourself out à la Paulette Goddard. If you are the 'Little Lake' type (size 9), you don't have to shop in the children's department and look like Alice in Wonderland. On the other hand, don't do yourself up like a poster; you're not tall enough to carry it. Also, if you are the Lake type, wear white as much as you can. Or monotone colors, pale gray, pale beige. In any event, stay away from fantastic prints and screaming color combinations. Small blondes can't carry them . . . they carry off small blondes . . . I don't build Veronica up—I have a phobia about being what you are and liking it, and emphasizing it. If you're short, don't try to

* "Dress Your Type," by Edith Head as told to Gladys Hall, *Screen-land*, XLVIII, No. 11 (September 1944), p. 33.

make yourself look tall; if you're tall, don't walk around as if you had the bends.

"To reverse the picture," she continued, carrying on her lesson and incidentally giving a good deal of information about her own methods of designing, "if you resemble Paulette Goddard you can go as mad as you like with colors . . . for Paulette *is* what we call the 'poster' type. She is vivid. She can stand the most sensational styles, the most fevered color combinations. She has so much vitality, she can dominate anything."

And "Because of that dominant, clean-cut, arresting quality, which is Barbara Stanwyck," Miss Head points out, "she has to be tailored morning, noon and night; must wear very un-trick clothes, nothing chi-chi. She has to put herself on the suit formula and stay with it. Betty Hutton is so blonde, *so* vivacious, she, too, must under-dress—in fact, *under*-under-dress, for at the mere drop of a spangle she would look *too* blonde, *too* pretty, *too* candy-box.

"These," the designer concluded, "are a few of the things I must know about the stars I dress; and you, in planning your own clothes, should know about yourselves. For *good clothes are not good luck*. They are the result of a pretty thoroughgoing knowledge of the people you are dressing. A knowledge not only of their measurements, coloring and facial contours, but, more importantly, of what makes them tick; of their characters. What you do with clothes is *counter-balance personality. Play it up or down*. So, as in every art and craft (this sounds pretty fancy, but it's true), you must have a working knowledge of your instrument before you can play upon it and produce harmonies."

But designing clothes for the movies is not, as I have already pointed out, just a matter of sticking to your period and to the style of your stars. There is the additional necessity of sticking to your story and not getting in its way. And that creates some of the most difficult problems of all. Not every woman in every movie is allowed to look her best and her prettiest. There are always the players who must portray such unattractive and unsympathetic roles as dowdy aunts and embittered old maids, and they have to be dressed to increase the effectiveness of their acting. For example, Miss Head once had to design a costume for Shirley Ross, when that actress was playing the part of a girl who was, according to the script, "a bit too smart." So Miss Head gave her a suit which she wouldn't recommend either to Miss Ross for her personal life, or to you. There were fur lapels on it, and enormous fur sleeves; and with it the actress wore a fur belt and a fur muff. Miss Head doesn't particularly enjoy devising costumes like that, but it's part of her job.

And sometimes she must deliberately design a dress that, if it is successful, will go unnoticed by the audience during the dramatic scene in which it is to be worn. Such a costume was once made for Louise Campbell to wear in "Men With Wings," for the sequence in which she was saying good-bye to her husband as he took off for the first trans-Atlantic airplane flight. It was a tense moment, and the attention of the audience must not be allowed to wander from the action to Miss Campbell's dress. To make matters worse, that particular picture was laid during a period when women wore low waistlines that look merely ludicrous to us today, so the dress Miss Head made had to be not only accurate for the era, but so especially unnoticeable that the audience would not be tempted to laugh at its old-fashioned lines.

No, Miss Head's job is never easy. But in spite of the fact that a person of less energy than hers would probably be in a constant state of nervous collapse under the pressure of so busy a schedule, Miss Head thinks that "designing for the pictures is the most exciting job in the world." Its everchanging personalities and problems are always a delight and a stimulation to her—and a list of the "personalities" with which she deals daily would alone seem to offer ample proof of this to most people. Among the stars she has dressed, often for their personal as well as their screen life, are Clara Bow, Mae West, Carole Lombard, Kay Francis, Gail Patrick, Madeleine Carroll, Luise Rainer, Joan Bennett, Shirley Temple, Claudette Colbert, Ilka Chase, Ida Lupino, Lupe Velez, Irene Dunne, Ingrid Bergman, Betty Grable, Hedda Hopper, Paulette Goddard, Ginger Rogers, Barbara Stanwyck, Dorothy Lamour, Mary Martin, Veronica Lake, Loretta Young, Olivia deHavilland, Joan Fontaine, Jennifer Jones, Gail Russell and Diana Lynn.

She says she had the "most fun" with Mae West—whose

FASHION IS OUR BUSINESS

Head-designed clothes, incidentally, once started a world-wide fashion—and Charles Laughton, whom she once had to dress as Nero.

And of course, as she hastens to add, she has fun at other things besides designing, too. She loves the ranch where she lives, and the enormous collection of masks and porcelain cats which she has picked up over a period of years. She likes the California sports of swimming and gardening, and the clothes she wears for them. Around the ranch she invariably wears comfortable slacks or full-skirted native costumes made of cloth she has woven for herself in Mexico.

Those clothes constitute by no means the only mark her childhood has left on her grown-up life. She still likes to visit Mexico, and goes every year if she can. She likes all Pan-American and Western and Indian fashions, and regards such Pan-American innovations as the *guayabera*, the *camisa* shirt, the *rebozo* scarf and the poncho as among her main contributions to Hollywood fashion.

She still speaks Spanish fluently, sends sketches frequently to South America, and broadcasts in Spanish over short-wave stations to South American women, because she has great confidence in the benefits to be derived from an increasingly closer relationship between the two continents of the Western Hemisphere.

And of course, she adds, she still has burros for pets. I was a little surprised when she said that, and asked her if she raised them for commercial purposes.

154

"Oh, no." Miss Head smiled. "Burros don't have any real commercial value in this country."

So I asked her what she *did* do with them.

"Why, we just keep them—except that once in a while we give one to a friend. And then, of course, after that the friend never speaks to us again."

She grinned when she said it, and I knew it was an exaggeration. But I decided that anybody who lives in such an exaggerated world as the movies, on the whole, constitute, and who keeps her sense of humor and her sense of reality as well as Miss Head does, was entitled to an exaggeration or two. And it pleased me, somehow, that burros were the thing she chose to exaggerate about.

TEN

—————LOUELLA BALLERINO—————

The year 1929 was one long and unpleasantly remembered in American history, as the beginning of a great financial depression. Businesses closed, men were put out of work, and lines in front of employment offices grew longer and more discouraged. There was scarcely an individual in the country who did not feel the effects of that disastrous downward swing of the economic cycle.

The young Melvin Ballerinos of Los Angeles, California, felt it too, and Mrs. Ballerino decided she ought at least to try to do something about their own personal predicament. She had been married for several years, she had two small children, and she hadn't worked since her graduation from the University of Southern California. But she was determined to do her share toward bolstering the family income.

It was easy enough to make up her mind where to start. As an undergraduate majoring in art and the history of art, she had frequently dashed off fashion sketches in her spare time. She had found them easy to do and tremendously lucrative. At a time when money wasn't particularly important to her, she had been able, between classes and dates, to earn a good sum of money. Now the memory of those handsome checks came back to her, with the determination to earn

LOUELLA BALLERINO

LOUELLA BALLERINO'S SKILLFUL ADAPTATION OF A RICH VARIETY OF AUTHENTIC NATIVE DESIGNS AND INFLUENCES GIVE HER CALIFORNIA=MADE PLAY CLOTHES A GAY WEAR=ABILITY.

COLORFUL EMBROIDERY FRO
A DISTANT LAND WAS THE INSPIRATION FOR LOUELL
BALLERINO'S PEASANT=SKIRTED PLAY FROCK, IN WHI(
AMERICAN GIRLS FEEL VERY MUCH AT HOME.

them again. She could still draw; in fact, she felt, she could undoubtedly draw better than she had, because now that money would mean a great deal indeed, and she would apply herself seriously to a task she had once regarded with youthful lightheartedness.

But Louella Ballerino discovered that she had yet to learn how widespread was the depression's influence. She found stores and wholesale houses who would buy her drawings all right, because they remembered her work in the past. But, they assured her, she mustn't expect to receive as much money as she had previously. No fashion artist, she was told, could make more than $125 a month now, no matter how many drawings she was willing to supply. If Louella was willing to work for that amount, employers would be glad to have her. If she wasn't—well, there were plenty of bright young girls who needed money, and who would leap at the chance.

So Mrs. Ballerino said she needed the money herself, even if it was far less than she had hoped for, and she agreed to the terms. And then she settled down to confer with herself about what else she could do. One advantage of making fashion sketches was that they could be done on one's own time, and Louella knew that she drew quickly. Therefore she would have time to earn her $125 a month, and work at something else as well. But what?

She sought advice and listened to it. It would be unwise, she was told, to attempt to branch out into some entirely new field. Fashion illustration was one thing she knew; why not, then, start with the training and ability she had, and add to it? There were other aspects of clothes that she knew nothing about, and she ought to educate herself along some of those lines. She ought, for example, to take courses in pattern-making and tailoring.

That didn't sound very exciting to a young matron eager to accomplish something immediately, but she recognized the soundness of it. So she enrolled for evening classes at the Frank Wiggins Trade High School in Los Angeles.

And then, still faced with the necessity for more money immediately, she found a full-time job for herself in a custom dress shop. There, every day, she had to pretend that she had no worries of her own at all, and was concerned only with the problems of wealthy customers unable to choose between one expensive dress and another. She showed them beautiful lengths of imported material, and sketched suggestions for gowns to be made from them in styles that would flatter figures and faces. Whenever a customer ordered one of Louella's designs, Louella received a $10 bonus.

It was an incredibly busy life she led, but it was to become even busier. After she had attended her evening classes for some time, her teachers found that she was very useful indeed when they needed sketches to illustrate some point in their lectures. She seemed to have a very real feeling for clothes, and they were amazed at how much she seemed to know about them. Louella confessed that she had always been interested in books on costume design, and had begun a small collection of them as a hobby. She had also, she admitted, studied textile design under Andre Ani, a Metro-Goldwyn-Mayer artist.

Consequently, when one of the teachers left, Louella was called into the principal's office one night and offered the job of teaching a class in fashion design and illustration. She was appalled at the thought of accepting such a responsibility, but it meant that her evenings too would bring in an income—although a small one, of course—and so she accepted.

For several years thereafter her schedule was one that would have terrified a husky Amazon. She got up early in the morning to look after her household duties and get her family ready for its day. Then she rushed off to the shop, where she spent wearing hours trying to please her employer and his customers, snatched something to eat for her dinner, and went on to the school. Her classes there were over at 9 o'clock, and she jumped into her car at one minute after nine each night to drive as rapidly as the speed laws permitted to the local library. That institution closed at ten, and Louella always had a great deal of research to do there in order to keep up with her students. The late night hours and week ends she devoted to her fashion sketches.

She admits now that she would probably never have the courage to undertake such a program again, but it seemed to her then the only thing to do—so she did it. She even adds, cheerfully, that everything fitted in very neatly, provided one only had the strength to keep going. She learned so much working with her classes, she explains, and striving desperately to contrive an effective lecture for them each evening, that her own designs for the custom shop inevitably improved. And fashion sketches, too, were often suggested by some ancient costume she had originally copied in the library to serve as what she called a "point of concentration" for her students the next night.

That "point of concentration" was the basis of her teaching, as it is today the basis of her own designing.

"I always told my students," she declares, "that they couldn't expect to be really original. After all, there are just so many colors in the world, and so many lines; and everything they could conceive of had, somewhere, sometime, been done before. Therefore what they must learn was, first, the ability to concentrate; and, next, the ability to adapt old ideas to new forms. Of course they must be constantly aware of the world about them, and of the general trend in which fashion was moving. But beyond that it was up to them to create new styles by applying their minds to the adaption of already-existing things."

Louella frequently brought some "already-existing thing" to class with her, and let the students make what they could of it. It might be an old costume print, or it might be something as surprising as a phonograph record, or a handful of colored paper scraps which she scattered at random on a plain gray surface. But whatever it might be, it would, she told them, if sufficient concentration was supplied, stir up some mental image or some emotion from which fashion ideas could emerge.

To Louella Ballerino that is still an almost fool-proof method for designing. Its only secret lies in the stubbornness of one's concentration and—this is just as important—the store of information in one's memory, from which bits and pieces can be pulled to elaborate upon the basic idea, once it has suggested itself.

Of course she did her best to furnish her students with information, as well as to train their minds to use it.

"I felt they should have a taste of everything," she says, "that there was nothing they could know too much about. I taught them color theory, both prismatic and pigmatic, and made arrangements with the school's life class for them to draw from live models one night a week. Today, when clothes are made for comfort, it's more important than ever to understand and know the human anatomy."

But sometimes, in spite of all her efforts, she arrived at school convinced that that evening she had nothing to say. Perhaps one of her children had taken sick and she had been up nursing most of the night; or perhaps she had fallen behind with her fashion sketches and had been unable to get to the library the evening before.

"When that happened," she says, "I deliberately wore bizarre clothes to class. I made all my own clothes, of course" —she doesn't bother to explain how she found time for that, along with everything else—"and they were, I admit, rather extreme. I don't know what my friends thought of my dresses in those days, but frequently a daring drapery line or a great clanking piece of jewelry served the purpose of distracting my students from the fact that I didn't have much to say. And sometimes they even gave the boys and girls ideas they could work with themselves."

Clearly neither the Board of Education nor her classes shared Louella's nervousness as to her teaching ability. As the Ballerino finances improved, Mr. Ballerino urged his wife to give up her teaching job, but no one wanted to let her go. Finally, at the end of five and a half years of that gruelling program, Mr. Ballerino had his way and Louella left. In the last year of her teaching her students won five of the six designing contests they had entered, and even today Louella Ballerino is a popular guest lecturer and a generous giver-of-advice to young students of design in her community.

In the meantime her own fashion-designing career was moving forward, but not always steadily. After several years at the custom shop she was offered a job at a higher salary, to design clothes for a wholesale house, and she accepted. But at the end of a few weeks one of the drawings for her new employer was scathingly criticized.

"Never turn in a sketch like this again," she was sternly warned. "The neckline is bad, the silhouette is bad, the sleeve is bad. It's all awful. Now let us have something we can use."

Louella went back to her workroom and stared at the drawing board. She had been proud of that dress. It had been unusual, she knew, but wasn't it her job to make things that were different? Wasn't that what she had been hired for? At the moment she couldn't imagine why she had been hired at all, and she felt her employers couldn't either.

For three days she struggled with her despair, unable even to draw a line. Each idea that came into her mind was discarded instantly, before she could put pencil to paper. Her bosses probably wouldn't like it, she told herself; so what was the use of sketching it at all?

And finally she gave up. She handed in her resignation and returned, defeated, to her old job.

And then, not long afterward, she discovered that that "bad" dress had been manufactured after all, and that it was one of the most successful models of the season. Her confidence was restored. But she gave herself a full additional year of experience before she accepted the next job that was offered. This time she didn't want to be fired.

This time she wasn't. On the contrary, her designs were so well received that, shortly afterward, she went into partnership with a friend and opened her own custom business. It was immediately and gratifyingly successful. It was, in fact, as far as Louella was concerned, almost too successful. Because she was receiving increasing orders for designs from wholesalers, and she no longer had time to do them. Forced to make up her mind where her principal interests lay, she eventually resigned from the new business and took a loft for herself, where she spent her full time sketching to order.

One of those sketches proved to be a turning point in her career. A manufacturer had ordered something "really different," and Louella, glad of the opportunity to put a few novel ideas into practice, gave him a sketch for a simple peasant-like dress. It was to be made in a rough hopsacking, with a wide turned-down collar embroidered in bright-colored wool, and a wide skirt decorated with a broad band of yarn figures embellished with squares of wood sewn into the embroidery. A sash belt held the skirt snugly in at the waist. Altogether it looked more as if it ought to be worn on the plains of middle Europe, than in a twentieth-century American town.

"It was a little crazy, I knew," Louella says. "But I thought it would be fun to wear, and comfortable."

As you will have imagined, the manufacturer who had ordered it didn't agree. He had said, "different," he pointed out; not "ridiculous." And he handed the drawing back with a frown.

On the previous occasion when that sort of thing had happened, Louella had been crushed. But now she remembered the success of that other discarded dress, and she decided she was right this time too. At any rate, she was willing to gamble on her rightness. She bought up bolts of hopsacking, hired a manufacturer to make the dress up, and asked permission to hang a few of the finished models in a Hollywood shop. The shop owner was reluctant, but Louella persisted. "Just let customers see them," she urged. "If they don't like them, I'll take them away immediately."

A few hours later the shop owner was clamoring for more. The dresses had been fairly snatched from his racks, he explained in some embarrassment, and friends of the first customers were already besieging the shop asking for copies for themselves.

As simply as that—if you can somehow manage to forget the years of struggle that went before—Louella Ballerino was in business, as a full-fledged designer, and the manufacturer of her own designs. For months that dress was one of the major fashion enthusiasms of the country, and its gay peasant characteristics were imitated by wholesale houses from coast to coast.

But the dress itself merits attention for other reasons than its popularity, and its effect on the Ballerino success-story. In several respects it was to set the trend for the wholesale business that it founded. For one thing, its material was a sturdy, rough-textured weave, resembling—for all its inexpensiveness—a hand-woven cloth. And Ballerino fashions have frequently since been made up in just such sturdy types of material, sometimes actually hand-woven ones, but in any case capable of taking the laundering and hard wear that is always demanded of action and play clothes by practical people.

For another thing, its full skirt was characteristic of many Ballerino styles-to-come. Louella eventually introduced the dirndl to California fashion markets, and has given it many of its gayest, most colorful interpretations.

And finally, but perhaps most importantly, that gay embroidery was a forerunner of the dozens of vivid adaptations of native designs that have become almost a trade-mark of Ballerino clothes. Those yarn figures on the hopsacking collar and skirt had been copied from a design originated by the Tongan tribe of Africa—and copied accurately.

The final word in that last paragraph deserves a whole new paragraph to itself. Accuracy in regard to her designs is a matter of great importance to Louella Ballerino. Her original meager collection of books on costume design has now increased to a truly impressive size, and she studies it constantly. She likewise studies in museums and galleries and history books, and whenever she has a chance she travels to further enlarge her sources. Every imaginable type of native art has been investigated, with the idea of adapting it to wearable American clothes, and every time she puts even the narrowest border around a cotton skirt, she is careful to be sure that its basic pattern is an accurate representation of the traditional one from which she derived it.

The uses to which she has put native materials are endlessly fascinating—and apparently fascinatingly endless. In 1938, the first year in which she was in business for herself, she put out a whole collection of frocks colorfully embroidered in Bulgarian peasant style. They had full skirts, gay peasant aprons, embroidered blouses and short jackets.

The next year she took the Dutch as her "point of concentration," for full-trousered Dutch-boy slacks, with short double-breasted jackets in a contrasting color. After that she borrowed some of the beautiful Aztec designs, and she has since similarly utilized Russian, Norwegian, Polish, Mayan, Chinese, American Indian, Mexican, Bolivian and other Latin-American patterns.

She always translates accurately from her originals, and always adapts freshly and with an amused, understanding sense of what Americans want to wear. Sometimes she borrows only an embroidery design from the native costume she has chosen to work with, and uses it to trim an otherwise simple and almost classic dress. Sometimes she borrows the actual lines of a costume, as she did with her Dutch collection and, later, for a series of Chinese-inspired fashions that were widely advertised and sold under the name of "Coolies." "Coolies" were simple frocks of rayon jersey in plain pale colors, trimmed only with bands of contrasting color around the edge of the short lotus sleeves and down the front surplice closing, and they expressed the feeling rather than the details of Chinese clothes. One of her most popular successes was the *pollera* collar from Panama; this wide, low-necked frill, decorated with painted flowers or lace, was borrowed in its entirety to form the focal point for a whole series of white-blouse-and-dark-skirt combinations.

And so it goes. Having chosen her "point of concentration" from the world's store of native arts, Louella Ballerino studies it and lives with it until it evokes a gay and wearable American fashion.

She has done something else, too, as influential to what we wear as her introduction of native themes. She has sponsored the mother-and-daughter clothes that have become an outstanding symbol of American styles. Mother-and-daughter dirndls, mother-and-daughter gardening clothes and play suits, one a tiny but perfect replica of the other, have been shipped out from the Ballerino workroom in Los Angeles to stores everywhere. And their popularity is a clear indication, it seems to me, of basic truths about American fashions and about Louella Ballerino herself.

On the one hand they suggest two beliefs increasingly widespread among our designers: that a child has as much right as her mother to a carefully-designed, carefully-executed dress; and that a mother is as much interested as her young daughter in clothes that are fun to wear, and that will stand up under the strain of active work and play.

And on the other hand they suggest, as clearly as Mrs. Ballerino's remarks about the "point of concentration," what sort of a person she is herself. She has a daughter of her own, and she regards her with all the respect she feels for another adult. She has instilled in her her own eagerness to search out beauty wherever it may be found, and her own determination to make that beauty a part of her own life and a contribution to the lives of others.

Mrs. Ballerino and Wanda went to Mexico together, and there they laughed over the same things, exclaimed over the same things and, between them, brought back a wealth of material. Louella returned with Mexican *rebozos*—vivid, multi-colored scarves—which served as the inspiration for a group of dresses; and Wanda had a bookful of sketches. Wanda is a sculptress, too, as her mother once hoped to be; and Mrs. Ballerino feels a deep sense of satisfaction and pride in that fact.

"Now I don't have to try so hard to find time for my own modeling any more," she says. "Wanda will be the sculptress instead."

Respect for her materials, and a great deal of hard work, have brought Louella Ballerino success, after a period of retirement from which many women would have been unable to force themselves, even stimulated by the economic necessity which first drove Mrs. Ballerino on. But she has never ceased to be a warmly active member of her family (she has a grown son, too, now in the Air Corps), no matter how demanding her business ventures became. She organizes parties around the outdoor grill in the patio of the Ballerino home, poses interminably for photographic experiments of her camera-enthusiast husband (he is a motion picture casting director, and Louella has done some work for the movie studios too, although she has never been interested in offers to design exclusively for the screen), and listens, with her family, to a great deal of music from their large record collection.

She has little time for active sports these days, but she is interested in them, as all Californians seem to be, and especially interested in the sort of clothes that make them more enjoyable. Her skate-and-ski fashions have appeared at all the most popular winter resorts in the land.

Artist and executive, wife and mother—Louella Ballerino's energy, imagination and enthusiasm make it possible for her to be all of them at once. She does more than most people, but constantly regrets that she hasn't time to do more. She is always planning trips she wants to take and new fields of enterprise she expects to experiment in. She is, for example, vitally concerned with the development of hand-weaving crafts in California—an art she believes will become increasingly important to the economy of the state, and to California's gay and colorful influence upon American clothes.

Those who know her take for granted that eventually she will go everywhere and accomplish everything she puts her mind to. Doing what she sets out to do seems to be a habit of hers.

ELEVEN

MARISKA KARASZ

Mariska Karasz thought her career as a designer was over when her daughter, Solveig, was born. She and her husband had talked it over, and they had decided that a child deserved and should receive a mother's full attention. But it was, paradoxically enough, just because Mariska was such a devoted mother that she found herself back at work all over again before long—this time fashioning clothes for her new baby. And when Rozsika was born, a few years later, doubling her mother's youthful clientele, Mariska Karasz was well on her way to becoming an outstanding designer in a specialized field. Today the play clothes and party dresses of almost every member of the youngest set from Maine to California show the influence, to some degree, of the gaiety and beauty and common sense which she first put into her own children's things.

Mariska was born in Budapest. Her small, dark-eyed, vivacious face and her deep respect for the arts of handicraft, were both bequeathed to her by her Hungarian forebears. Her father was a silversmith, and the Karasz children—there were three of them, two girls and a boy—were matter-of-factly expected to be able to make beautiful things with their hands.

FASHION IS OUR BUSINESS

The Budapest public schools expected it too. From the time Mariska entered her first classroom, at the age of five, until she finished the Hungarian equivalent of an American high school at fifteen, she spent a great many of her school hours sewing. She learned to take stitches so tiny that, looking at them today, she wonders how her eyes could see to make them. She learned to pull threads to keep endless tucks absolutely straight, and she did elaborate embroidery and intricate crocheting.

I said that the Budapest schools expected children to be good at the manual arts, but Mariska was really rather especially good. Her teachers recognized it, and so did her family. When an uncle from America came on a visit one day and asked his nieces what skill each of them excelled at, they could answer without question. Ilonka, the elder sister, was best at art (she was eventually so clever at drawing that she became one of the first girls to be admitted to the Imperial Arts and Crafts School), and Mariska was best at sewing.

She always took advantage of the regular visits of her mother's seamstress, to watch how real grown-up clothes were made, and to help plan her own dresses. She says now that she fears she was perhaps too vocal about what she wanted, and too demanding about getting it.

The Karasz family lived the greater part of each year in Budapest itself, but they spent their summers in the country, and the children grew up with a sense of the great excitement

CLARA E. SIPPRELL

MARISKA KARASZ

DISSATISFIED WITH READY=MADE CHILDREN'S CLOTHES, MARISKA KARASZ RETURNED TO A CAREER ABANDONED AT HER DAUGHTER'S BIRTH, AND WON A NEW REPUTATION DESIGNING FOR THE VERY YOUNG.

SOLVEIG AND ROZSIKA CHOSE
THEIR OWN TRIMMING FOR DRESSES WHICH THEIR MOTHER
MARISKA KARASZ, MADE FOR THEM (AND THEIR DOLLS)
FROM A SINGLE SIMPLE PATTERN.

in nature and in growing things themselves, that so many city-bred youngsters lack. It was a peaceful, pleasant life. But unfortunately Mr. Karasz died when Mariska was small, and eventually the girls' mother came to the United States. She wanted her son and daughters to finish school in their native country, but as they were graduated she sent for them, one by one, to join her in New York.

By the time Mariska arrived here, she already knew that she wanted to work with clothes, in some way or other. She had been making exquisite blouses for herself, and for her sister. And soon friends of the family asked Mariska to make blouses for them too. Sometimes she had more ambitious and dramatic ideas. If she saw a particularly fetching picture of a French soldier in a history book, she attempted to design and construct a suit for herself along the lines of that intricately-cut costume. She says the results might have looked a little bizarre, but to her own eyes it was well-made and therefore beautiful—and in her opinion she grew and learned by the very process of attempting something that was admittedly beyond her.

In what proved to be a misguided effort to increase her education along the path she was most interested in, she took a course at a drafting school, where she studied the drafting of patterns. But the classes were limited in their application to the broad field of designing, and, feeling that she wasn't deriving sufficient benefit from them, she left at the end of six months.

173

Fashion is our Business

Next she attended Cooper Union Art School, and there she was fortunate enough to study under Miss Ethel Traphagen, who was later to found the Traphagen School of Design.

"I drew rather badly," Miss Karasz says, "and when Miss Traphagen took a sketch from my desk to hold it up in front of the class for criticism, I would be terribly embarrassed. But instead of pointing out its defects, she would say, 'Doesn't this show a fine originality?'"

Her teacher's ability to see, in even the most awkward drawing, the one thing that distinguished it; and her sympathetic encouragement of that one trait, without too much dwelling upon Mariska's failings, were of tremendous help in guiding her progress.

When she left school she decided to capitalize, if she could, on the one achievement that had earned her most praise in the past. So she made up several of her loveliest blouses and took them to Wanamaker's New York store, where they were bought by the department specializing in French importations. There they sold so well that the store soon suggested that they be given a department of their own. So Mariska was hired at a definite salary—but on a part-time basis, because she was still very young—and two assistants were taken on to work out the designs she prepared.

Shortly afterward M. D. C. Crawford, of the trade newspaper, *Women's Wear*, became interested in the application of authentic American designs to American fashions, and he called together a group of designers—including Mariska—and invited them to work out his plan. She says that the research she did with that group was one of the most interesting experiences of her life. Museums allowed the designers to study actual historic garments, and contemporary styles were worked out directly from those carefully-preserved clothes.

In the meantime an opening occurred in Jessie Franklin Turner's department at Bonwit Teller, and Mariska was asked to fill it. Her first assignment there, she recalls with amusement, was to design a bathing suit with trousers that came below the knee, and with long sleeves. But even such restrictions couldn't completely bury her originality, and soon Bonwit Teller was presenting a window display featuring beach clothes designed by Mariska, and based on adaptations of Indian patterns which she had discovered during her museum research.

She liked her job on the whole, and realized that she was lucky to be so well situated, considering her youth and the brief time she had been in America. But when a Hungarian friend of hers opened a small new shop on Eighth Street, in downtown New York, and invited Mariska to display some of her things there, the girl seized upon the opportunity as a possible doorway to the one thing her job didn't give her: independence. She made up a group of blouses trimmed with imported embroidery and appliqué, and they were sold almost as soon as they appeared on the counter. At the end of a year Mariska felt justified in resigning her job and opening her own studio on Madison Avenue, with a seamstress to help her.

Looking back, she marvels at the daring that prompted her to take such a step. With supreme self-assurance, she merely sent out announcements of her opening, and waited for the customers to come. Fortunately, they came. People had seen Mariska's work in the stores, and they were willing to climb even the long flights of stairs to her place, to have the opportunity of buying it again. They were frequently amazed to see so youthful-looking a girl open the door to them, and more than one woman asked Mariska kindly, "Is your mother at home?" But they bought her clothes, and that was what mattered.

As soon as she could afford it, Mariska made a trip to Europe and sought out various gifted Hungarian craftsmen who could execute the kind of embroidered and appliquéd designs she wanted. She never had the garments themselves fashioned for her abroad, because she felt that only in this country could they be given the styling that American women wanted; but she had lengths of material decorated there, and sent to the United States to be made up in her own studio.

Her reputation grew steadily, and before she had been at work many years she was recognized as the source of a particular kind of exquisite workmanship, featuring native handwork, that was seldom obtainable in this country. Finally she took a collection of her blouses and dresses to the West

Coast, to exhibit them there—and that was where she met young Donald Peterson, then a naval lieutenant.

The third time she saw him, he proposed to her. She scarcely liked to say yes on such short acquaintance, but she knew irrevocably that she was going to say yes eventually. And she knew that if she didn't say it then, he would simply have to follow her east when she returned home and ask her again. She is a direct and realistic person, so she thought such a long trip would be a waste of time and money if it could be avoided. Mariska agreed to marry him immediately. He managed a ten-day leave, which allowed them a week's honeymoon after they had waited the required three days between the issuance of the license and the performance of the ceremony. And then she went back to New York and her husband remained in California to tie up the loose ends of his work so that he might resign and join her.

Mariska didn't realize right away that marriage was going to affect her career. With her husband's full approval she carried on in her studio for some time. But then Solveig was born—and we have brought the story up to the point with which we began it, in the first paragraph.

Mariska didn't particularly want to design clothes any more. She enjoyed Solveig very much, and was perfectly content to spend her days with this very individual young daughter she had brought into the world. Solveig, named by her Swedish father, was a sturdy baby, with an early tendency to explore the world around her. And when Mariska went shopping for her, she was repeatedly dissatisfied with the clothes she had to buy. They were, for the most part, of pale delicate voiles, trimmed with lace or tiny rosebuds—and Solveig simply wasn't that kind of a baby.

So, without thinking very much about it at first, Mariska ran up a few things for her herself. They were the sort of clothes she thought suited Solveig. They were gay, colorful, sturdy overalls of challis or other long-wearing material; or tiny sun suits that allowed a maximum of freedom and a maximum of exposure to the sun. They were easy to get into, and it wasn't very long before Solveig was dressing herself. And, besides, Solveig loved them.

And then, pretty soon, there was Roszika. And Roszika had to have things made especially for her too.

By that time Mariska had worked out a fairly clear philosophy of clothes for young children. They had to be comfortable, of course. They had to be easy to handle—and that meant not only easy to get into and out of, but easy to wash and iron. They had to be sturdy, so that a mother didn't feel compelled at every other moment to tell her child to be careful, or to pick her up off the floor for fear she would ruin whatever she had on. They had to be individualized to suit the particular child. And, by no means least important, they had to be fun to wear: they must be gay in color, and gay in spirit too. Mariska could never see any reason why even a very young child shouldn't find the same thrill in her clothes that her mother found in a new spring dress.

Perhaps it all sounds rather complicated, written out like that, but it wasn't so in practice. Very simple clothes, provided only that they were made from the right materials and with careful workmanship, could just as easily have all those attributes as not. And, what's more, they were as pleasant for the mother as they were for the child, if they did. They were more fun to make, for one thing, if a mother made her child's own clothes; and it was certainly more amusing for a mother to see her daughter toddling around in a tiny sun suit whose funny pocket enchanted her, than to watch her struggling with a froth of voile that got in her way every time balance required a quick clutch at a near-by chair leg.

In fact, Mariska's philosophy made so much sense that other people who heard about it were impressed. One day, talking quite casually to a friend about the whole business, she found herself being urged to design a collection of clothes according to her principles for Bamberger's big store in Newark, N. J. Mariska furnished the designs, and the store had them manufactured. When they appeared they caused a great deal of excitement and Mariska found she had won an entirely new kind of reputation for herself as a designer.

Later on, Saks Fifth Avenue store in New York promoted a collection of her designs. That was a particularly happy experience, because the clothes were shown in connection with a series of nursery rooms decorated and planned by Mariska's sister, Ilonka, who was by that time fully justifying her early promise as an artist.

FASHION IS OUR BUSINESS

Finding herself in business again, Mariska had to choose between the two possibilities of selling her designs to manufacturers or pattern-makers; and keeping her production on a small custom scale which she could handle herself. After some consideration she chose the latter. She had always preferred to have her own place, and to see a job through from start to finish. And she had learned that it was usually necessary to compromise to some extent when she attempted to meet the requirements of wholesalers accustomed to dealing in thousands of dozens of garments, and consequently unwilling to risk anything that deviated very far from already-accepted styles. She has at various times done designs that have been widely reproduced, and she says that such work is more satisfactory now than it was in the past; because now the whole manufacturing world—and the world of mothers, too—accept without question most of the basic principles of sturdiness and color which were, only a little while ago, regarded as outlandish.

She found her custom work, however, almost pure pleasure. Every child who was brought to her was a stimulation and a challenge, and could be given the same individualized attention which an expensive couturier lavishes upon a beautiful woman. One thing the children especially loved about their Mariska Karasz clothes was the fact that each of them had a name. There was the "Lady Bug" dress, with huge replicas of its insect inspiration for pockets; the "Purple Cow," with an appliqué of that fabulous animal surrounded by flowers; "A-Tisket, A-Tasket," whose bloom-like buttons seemed to spill out of a flower basket; "It Is Raining," with long drops splashing diagonally from top to bottom; and the fascinating "Go Away" dress, on which coaches and an engine traveled a never-ending journey around the hem. Mariska believed that every dress should be an adventure; and the joy with which her young customers received their "adventures," seemed to prove that they had long felt that way about it too, and were grateful to find a grown-up who actually understood their sentiments on the subject.

Mariska's prices were high, necessarily, because her dresses were made largely by hand, and each one was an "original" created with loving care and imagination. But even people who objected to those prices at first, returned later to report happily that the dress which had seemed so expensive had already paid for itself by long wear, and was now being cherished by a younger sister or a younger cousin of the child for whom it had been bought. Probably few artists or craftsmen have the experience of seeing their productions regarded as heirlooms during their own lifetime; but that is just what Mariska's clothes are in many families. And even when several "generations" of active children inherit and wear them, they remain colorful and sturdy—and fun.

As Solveig and Roszika grew older, they continued to be their mother's principal inspiration, and eventually they became real participants in the Karasz enterprises. They learned to sew for themselves, and their ventures into what their mother taught them to see as the truly exciting world of needle-and-thread finally resulted in a book. *See and Sew,** by Mariska Karasz, was written with the very active aid of Solveig and Roszika, who tested all the instructions in this book for young needlewomen, and indeed even originated some of them themselves. And they, in turn, had the eager assistance of other girls in the neighborhood, who begged to be allowed to join the wonderful sewing sessions that took place on the lawn of the Peterson country house in Brewster, N. Y.

The best thing about sewing under Miss Karasz's direction, they all felt, was that she didn't keep telling them that the thing they most wanted to make was "too hard" for a beginner. Mariska could remember those elaborate suits she had once designed for herself after pictures in her history books, and she realized that if some too-sensible grown-up had prevented her from working out her own ideas, she might have been discouraged forever from the whole idea of sewing and designing as a career.

So she allows her memory to dictate her advice to young sewers. You might be interested in some of that advice, either for your own benefit or for the assistance of a very young seamstress in your family.

"Give a child bright new material instead of an old dull garment to cut up and sew on, if you expect her to get any

* *See and Sew*, Mariska Karasz, J. B. Lippincott, New York, 1943.

pleasure out of her efforts," she says. "Let a little girl design her own patterns if she prefers. Children have so much imagination. I've found that little girls don't like aimless sewing. The finished article must—well, be able to go somewhere and do something. I remember when I was a child I used to watch my aunts sewing on samplers. Their work was exquisite. But they never got around to sewing anything else. Our children today aren't made that way."

If the youngest in your family is still too tiny to make even a single stitch for herself, you might, Miss Karasz suggests, want to try your hand at designing and making something for her. Her own story proves that such an adventure can be both pleasurable and profitable—for the maker as well as for the one who is to wear it.

TWELVE

MABS OF HOLLYWOOD
and
SUEDES BY VORIS

Mabs of Hollywood and Voris each started business with an idea—and very little else. And beyond the facts that they both live in California, that each uses her first name as a trade-mark (her real name, in both cases), and that both of them are successful, their stories have nothing in common except this: they both prove that specialization in the designing world is possible and profitable, provided one's specialty is based on a sound principle and exploited by a great deal of hard work. So I went to see them both, because specialization is likely to become more and more important in this field, and I thought you'd be interested in more than one example of a-single-idea-and-how-it-grew.

Let's take Mabs of Hollywood first. She makes bathing suits and foundation garments, and that's all. She wouldn't have time to manufacture other varieties of clothes even if she particularly wanted to, and as a matter of fact she doesn't. She has found that there are endless variations of even this simple theme, and she expects to spend a lifetime working them out.

Like a lot of other people whose business is specialized,

MABS

MABS WAS A DANCER WHEN CONCERN OVER THE FIT OF HER PRACTICE CLOTHES LAUNCHED HER ON A CAREER DEVOTED TO THE PRODUC= TION OF BATHING SUITS AND UNDERGARMENTS DESIGNED FOR FREEDOM OF MOVEMENT.

MANY AND INTRICATE A
THE SEAMS IN THE SIMPLEST BATHING SUIT BY MABS
HOLLYWOOD, BUT EACH IS NECESSARY FOR THE FIT AI
FREEDOM THE DESIGNER DEMANDS.

MABS AND VORIS

Mabs didn't start out in a large field and gradually narrow it down. She was never interested in designing as a whole, but only in her particular aspect of it. And her interest in that derived from quite another source.

She was a dancer. Even as a little girl, and long before she'd had a single dancing lesson, Mabs Elizabeth Ryden thought of herself as a dancer and believed firmly that dancing was the only career she could ever care for. But she had been born in Big Spring, Texas, and moved from there with her family when she was eight years old to Portland, Oregon —and Big Spring and Portland offered scant encouragement to a little girl with such a frivolous ambition. So did her father, a practical-minded contractor, and her two older brothers.

Eventually the family moved to Mount Shasta, California, where Mabs finished high school, and they then moved again to Hollywood. Still she hadn't had a dancing lesson, and Mabs was almost grown-up. In Hollywood, however, her luck turned. Here she found a lot of girls with ambitions similar to her own, and one day several of them whom she had met at the Studio Club confided in her that they had had a call from the Central City casting agency where they were registered. They were going to be auditioned for the chorus of a new Warner Brothers' picture. They asked if Mabs wanted to come too.

Mabs wasn't registered, of course—she had had no experience to offer the agency. But she went along anyway, and somehow—the movies were younger then, and not quite so hedged about with regulations as they are today—somehow she was allowed to try out. Probably the director thought she looked like a dancer, and so she did. She had a slender, rounded figure, graceful from long hours of sports and active games, and bright red curls bobbing over a pair of bright blue eyes. Those eyes were brighter than ever when the director's finger singled her out as one of the girls he had chosen.

Perhaps if Mabs had ever had a job before, she would have given that one up at the end of the first day. She had been designated as a wood sprite, and issued a thin filmy bit of gauze to wear. The weather was freezing and the wood sprites had to dance in the open air. It wasn't much fun. But even shivering flesh and chattering teeth couldn't discourage her. She was dancing, as she had always known she would, and in a real picture, starring the famous Corinne Griffith. She wouldn't have quit for the world.

She might have been fired, of course. But the steps weren't difficult, and Mabs caught on quickly, working with intense concentration. The director never discovered that he had hired a girl whose only previous audience had been her own reflection in a mirror.

As soon as the picture was finished, Mabs spent the money she had earned to take some dancing lessons. Her dancing teacher helped her to get her next job, this time at Universal.

And when James Cruze was making "The Great Gabbo," Mabs had a real solo part, performing acrobatics on a rope web one hundred feet above the ground. It wasn't the first time nor the last that she had to make courage serve as a substitute for experience. After that she had assignments in Eddie Cantor's "Kid from Spain" and "Palmy Days," and finally she won a stock contract at Metro-Goldwyn-Mayer. Mabs was convinced that her career was well on its way, and that it would go forward in the direction she had always imagined for it. Her bright eyes would have stared unbelievingly if anybody had told her that her real career hadn't even begun—and that dancing would prove to be only the springboard for it.

The way things happened was that she began to worry about the fit of her dancing costume. Most dancers worried about the same thing and, like Mabs, regretted the fact that when tights were as snug as they had to be, they were likewise extremely uncomfortable and restricting to easy movement. But, unlike Mabs, the others seemed to regard that fact as they did bad weather: a subject for complaint rather than action. Mabs thought maybe something could be done about it.

The chief difficulty with the tights, she decided, was that they had a seam down the middle, from front to back. There was no elasticity in a seam, and elasticity was what was needed. There was, of course, no elasticized cloth in those days, but Mabs finally reached the conclusion that material cut on the bias would allow for at least a small amount of stretching; and that seams placed elsewhere than through the middle of the garment would permit full advantage to be taken of that stretch. She wanted to make another change, too; she felt that although the tights couldn't be shortened in back, they could be curved a little higher to fit the curve of the thigh in front, and thus allow the thigh muscles free action without offending the dictates of modesty.

Mabs didn't know anything about sewing; she only knew what she wanted. So she took her suggestions to Inez Schrodt, one of the wardrobe mistresses, and together they worked them out. The minute Mabs put on the garment that resulted, she knew she had been right. Freedom of movement was what she had been aiming for, and she had achieved it.

Immediately all the other dancers on the lot were jealous. They wanted tights like that too. Eventually the studio made Mabs' design a part of its official wardrobe.

Mabs would have let it go at that. But, not long afterward, she realized that her contract at MGM was approaching its conclusion, and she became alarmed. Nobody ever knew whether a contract would be renewed or not, until the last moment. And right then Mabs couldn't risk being out of work, even for a little while. Her mother was sick, and needed care. And suppose the contract *wasn't* renewed?

Mabs thought it over and made up her mind. She would make arrangements right away so that, whatever happened, she would be assured of some kind of an income.

BARNABA

VORIS

VORIS'S SUITS, COATS AND DRESSES FASHIONED OF SOFT, RAINBOW=HUED SUEDES HAVE LIFTED THAT ONE=TIME SPORTS MATERIAL INTO THE REALM OF HIGH FASHION, AND HER NAME INTO THE ROSTER OF SUC= CESSFUL DESIGNERS.

RADIO PICTURES, INC.

VORIS MAKES EVENING DRESSES
THAT MUST BE TOUCHED AS WELL AS SEEN TO CONVINCE
ONESELF THAT THEY ARE OF SUEDE RATHER THAN OF
SOME ESPECIALLY SUPPLE FABRIC.